A DARING PROMISE

A DARING PROMISE

A Spirituality of
Christian Marriage

REVISED AND EXPANDED EDITION

RICHARD R. GAILLARDETZ

Liguori/Triumph
LIGUORI, MISSOURI

Imprimi Potest: Thomas D. Picton, C.Ss.R.
Provincial, Denver Province • The Redemptorists

Published by Liguori/Triumph • An imprint of Liguori Publications
Liguori, Missouri • www.liguori.org

Library of Congress Cataloging-in-Publication Data
Gaillardetz, Richard R., 1958–
   A daring promise : a spirituality of Christian marriage / Richard R. Gaillardetz. — Rev. and expanded ed.
      p. cm.
   Includes bibliographical references.
   ISBN 978-0-7648-1559-1
   1. Marriage—Religious aspects—Catholic Church. 2. Catholic Church—Doctrines. I. Title.
   BX2250 .G32 2007
   248 .4—dc22   2006035128

Printed in the United States of America
16 15 14 13 12 / 8 7 6 5 4
Revised edition 2007

TO DIANA,
MY TRUE COMPANION

CONTENTS

PREFACE

This book is not about how to make marriage easier. It will not make your marriage more romantic, your sex more passionate, your arguments fewer. It will not tell you how to "rekindle the love you've lost." It will offer few tips on improving your marriage. This book tells why faithful, committed marriage is difficult, why it is one of the most demanding endeavors one could undertake in our world today. I offer a series of reflections, guided by the wisdom of the Christian tradition, on why the "hardness" of committed marriage should not surprise us. The short answer is this: it is hard because, for the vast majority of Christians, marriage and family is the place where, by God's grace, we work out our salvation.

The marital commitment that a man and a woman make to each other before God and in the midst of the Christian community is a most perilous undertaking; it is a journey fraught with risk. Marriage offers the daring proposition that two people might unconditionally bind themselves together for life without destroying each other, their offspring, or both in the process. To promise oneself to another before God is, I am convinced, one of the most radical things we do as Christians.

I am very much at home within my own Roman Catholic tradition. Still, I think that my tradition has been reluctant to explore the particular way in which the call to holiness that we all receive at our baptism is realized within the context of faithful married life. As Mary Anne McPherson Oliver has observed, a quick perusal of those who have been canonized by the Catholic Church, and thereby elevated as models of holiness, promises little insight into marital spirituality: "The only married saints canonized in the twentieth century have been martyrs or stigmatics, widow/foundresses of religious orders, and husbands who left wife and family to become missionaries or hermits."[1] We have alarmingly few canonized saints who lived out a sexually active committed Christian marriage. This disparity says much about the gap between rhetoric and reality in Catholicism's position on marriage as a path to holiness.

Almost two decades into this hazardous adventure, I have learned just enough to remain humbled by the journey of Christian marriage. What I do know is that my commitment to my wife, Diana, was and is the most important single commitment I have made in my life. Writing about this commitment is itself a risky prospect as I have by no means mastered the virtues that this commitment demands. This book is something of a pilgrim's journal in which I reflect on the spiritual topography of the marriage relationship. The landscape I know best, however, is that which I have encountered in my own marriage. As lovely and beguiling and, yes, daunting as that particular countryside is, it belongs to our own marital journey and not that of any other. Yet I hope that other married couples, and those wishing to learn more about married life, might find in these pages some insight to help them along their own pilgrimage. If by way of these pages they cultivate a heightened attentiveness to both the beautiful scenery and the rugged terrain they must negotiate along the way, I will judge this book a great success. Marriage is only one of many possible ways for Christians to live their lives as a response to Christ's call to follow him. When marriage is lived out faithfully, it ought to offer the Church a public witness to the life of discipleship to which all Christians are called. To that extent I would hope that single persons and those called to lifelong celibacy might also derive some value from these reflections.

What follows is an exploration in marital spirituality. I do not pretend to offer a comprehensive theology of marriage. For that, readers would do well to look to reliable works by Michael Lawler, Theodore Mackin, and others.[2] Rather, it is my desire to bring two different perspectives into conversation: (1) a theologically informed view of marriage that is faithful to the deep wisdom of our Christian tradition, and (2) an honest reading of the lived experience of marriage with all of its joys and struggles. An authentic spirituality of marriage will be effective to the extent that it emerges from this kind of conversation.

The first chapter attends to the cultural forces that shape our understanding and practice of married life today. Many of the difficulties that couples face in remaining faithful to their marriage commitment are not due to any moral failing but are rather the consequence of living in a culture that is inhospitable to keeping commitments of any kind.

The second chapter explores some basic faith convictions that can provide a foundation for a spirituality of marriage. These convictions are often presented in technical and abstract language and therefore seem irrelevant to a practical spirituality. I make the case that, quite to the contrary, basic convictions about Jesus and the Trinity, for example, have tremendous significance for ordinary Christian living.

The third chapter reflects on my perception of marriage as an invitation into the life of communion to which all are called. What is distinctive about marriage, I believe, is the public witness to this life of communion. To marry, at least from a Christian perspective, is to make our marital relationship the concern of the Church and a gift to the world. We commit ourselves to be a visible sign of what it means to live in communion with God and neighbor. Frightening though it may sound, we are called to become *martyrs,* witnesses to a distinctive view of human life and fulfillment.

The fourth chapter turns to how marriage stands as a summons to conversion; indeed, the marriage relationship becomes that privileged place wherein married couples work out their salvation. In marriage we enter into the dying and rising of Christ as we embrace our spouse as more than the source for the fulfillment of our needs and desires—our spouse is also the mysterious "other" who cajoles and sometimes demands our growth. The connection between marriage and salvation is important. In North America we encounter strong forces that would privatize religion. Yet for Christians, salvation is never a private undertaking. We are creatures made for relationship, and our salvation can never be divorced from the web of relationships in which we live and realize our humanity. God's saving work is effected in and through our relationships with others. For those who submit to the saving pedagogy of marriage, the social context of salvation is felt all the more acutely.

The fifth chapter addresses the question of marital sexuality and finds inspiration in a rereading of the familiar story of the creation of man and woman in the Book of Genesis. We discover that the heart of human sexuality lies in our capacity for vulnerability and transparency before another. The connections between marriage and sexuality are strong and complex. Here Christians are confronted with the ambiguity of our own religious tradition. It is a tradition that has affirmed the sacredness of the marriage covenant even as it has been unable to purge a persistent suspicion about the intrinsic goodness of sexuality. Within Catholicism, the theological significance of conjugal relations has swung like a pendulum between two extremes. Great voices in our tradition have been inclined to limit the goodness of marital sex to childbearing and a "remedy to concupiscence." It should be remembered, however, that these perspectives, harsh and pessimistic by modern standards, often moderated far more extreme denunciations of sexuality. In the past fifty years the pendulum has swung in the opposite direction. Catholic literature, including many official Church documents, is quick to speak of the theological meaning and beauty of marital sex, but in such highly romanticized language that many couples find little connection between this lofty prose and what they experience in their bedrooms.

In the sixth chapter I consider marriage as the establishment of a community of the home, what Roman Catholic literature has begun to refer to as the "domestic church." This provides an opportunity to consider the relationship between marriage and

Christian mission, as well as the gift and challenge of parenthood within the marriage relationship.

Though I take complete responsibility for what appears on these pages, there is an obvious sense in which my wife, Diana, is the coauthor of this volume. Although the words and overarching structure are mine, the wisdom, such as it is, is the shared fruit of a journey we have taken together. I am grateful that she has trusted me enough to allow our marriage to be mined for insight in these pages. Our four boys, David, Andrew, Brian, and Gregory, are now old enough to grasp something of what it means to say that "Dad is writing a book." Yet until sports heroes, astronauts, or wizards find their way onto these pages, my sons are likely to remain unimpressed. For this, too, I am grateful; they are often my surest anchor as I float adrift on a sea of theological musings.

I have been blessed with many friends with whom I have been able to reflect on the gifts and challenges of married life. Among these I must single out Rob Wething, whose honesty, integrity, vulnerability, and sense of humor have been an immeasurable gift to me. My dear friends, Mary Comeaux and Kevin O'Brien, taught me so much about genuine human relationships and, I am confident, they continue to offer their support as they abide among the blessed in heaven.

At a difficult time in our marriage, Diana and I found solace and support in the wise and tender arms of a married couple, Winnie and Wally Honeywell, who were wonderful mentors for us. Our own halting insights were often confirmed, refined, and developed in their honest testimony. Our good fortune in being able to count them as friends and guides also serves as an admonishment to the Church: we desperately need married mentors to help young couples stay the course.

I must also acknowledge those who graciously offered constructive commentary on early drafts of this work: Sidney Callahan, John Cockayne, Michael Downey, Fran Ferder, John Heagle, Winnie Honeywell, Nicki Maddox, John Rooney, and David Thomas. I want to express my gratitude to those at Crossroad Publications who helped bring the first edition of this volume to print, and to the editorial leadership at Liguori Publications, including Danny Michaels, Father Harry Grile, Hans Christoffersen, and Alicia von Stamwitz, for their support and editorial assistance in publishing this revised and expanded edition.

RICHARD R. GAILLARDETZ
MURRAY/BACIK PROFESSOR OF CATHOLIC STUDIES
UNIVERSITY OF TOLEDO
SEPTEMBER 2006

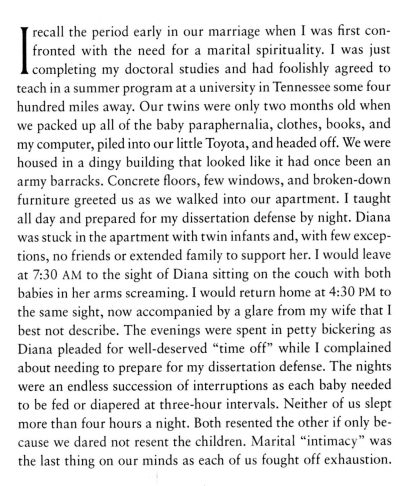

Chapter One

MARRIAGE AND CULTURE

I recall the period early in our marriage when I was first confronted with the need for a marital spirituality. I was just completing my doctoral studies and had foolishly agreed to teach in a summer program at a university in Tennessee some four hundred miles away. Our twins were only two months old when we packed up all of the baby paraphernalia, clothes, books, and my computer, piled into our little Toyota, and headed off. We were housed in a dingy building that looked like it had once been an army barracks. Concrete floors, few windows, and broken-down furniture greeted us as we walked into our apartment. I taught all day and prepared for my dissertation defense by night. Diana was stuck in the apartment with twin infants and, with few exceptions, no friends or extended family to support her. I would leave at 7:30 AM to the sight of Diana sitting on the couch with both babies in her arms screaming. I would return home at 4:30 PM to the same sight, now accompanied by a glare from my wife that I best not describe. The evenings were spent in petty bickering as Diana pleaded for well-deserved "time off" while I complained about needing to prepare for my dissertation defense. The nights were an endless succession of interruptions as each baby needed to be fed or diapered at three-hour intervals. Neither of us slept more than four hours a night. Both resented the other if only because we dared not resent the children. Marital "intimacy" was the last thing on our minds as each of us fought off exhaustion.

Somewhere during those four weeks the thought began to creep into each of our minds that our marriage was a horrible mistake. This is not what we bargained for, what we stayed up until the late hours fantasizing about in the heady days of our engagement. There, little more than two years into our marriage, we found ourselves staring into the abyss.

I believe that many couples come to such a point in their relationship. It is the point when the relationship stops being effortless and becomes work, work that can feel exhausting and futile. We survived that summer, though to this day I am not sure how. There was no great epiphany or profound experience that constituted the clear turning point. Call it the grace of the sacrament if you wish; all I know is that we began working harder to voice our resentments and frustrations directly to each other.

The image that comes to my mind for what began to happen in our relationship is drawn from a childhood memory of being on the stern of a large river boat, mesmerized by the soothing movement of the paddlewheel churning up the murky river water as it propelled the boat upstream. As we approached the dock, the pilot shifted the engine into reverse. The paddlewheel's steady rhythm diminished, slowly coming to a stop, and then, after a discernible pause, the wheel only gradually and with the utmost of effort began to turn in the opposite direction. That summer saw a gradual but real reversal in the cycle of our own relations. The pattern of caustic complaints and sarcastic responses slowly gave way to a new pattern of care toward each other. The difficulties did not disappear, but each of us seemed to recognize, beyond our own pain and frustration, the effort our spouse was putting forth, and that mutual recognition triggered a reversal.

As I reflect on that difficult time, it has become clear to me that an authentic spirituality of marriage is forged at the intersection of our contemporary culture and religious faith. Many of the difficulties that Diana and I experienced in Tennessee were a direct consequence of the cultural shape of our lives. Our marriage has not been lived in a vacuum. We live within a particular culture that exerts a certain force on us and predisposes us to interpret our lives in very specific ways.

The Impact of North American Culture on Married Life Today

It is tempting to consider the many problems with marriage in today's society and locate the origins of these problems in some central moral failing. "People simply aren't as committed to marriage as they once were," we tell ourselves. "Nobody is willing to sacrifice anymore." The underlying assumption seems to be that if people were simply more courageous, more virtuous, more committed, we would not be having this marriage crisis. I am not convinced that things are quite that simple. I believe most people, for example, enter into marriage fully expecting it to be a lifelong commitment. They do not, by and large, plan to divorce. What is different today from the situation of marriage some fifty years ago is our cultural landscape. In my analysis, I will draw considerably from the perceptive study of David Matzko McCarthy, author of *Sex and Love in the Home*.[1] Let us consider five features of our contemporary cultural landscape that make sustaining a marriage commitment difficult: (1) our cultural obsession with romance and passion, (2) the myth of "the right one," (3) the impact of our consumer culture, (4) therapy as a model for marriage, and (5) changing conceptions of the household in America.

Our Cultural Obsession With Romance

Romantic literature has a long and distinguished pedigree. But contemporary North American culture seems to have an obsession with romance that is new in several respects. It is an obsession fed by the influence of Hollywood and television. Our culture grants a startling power to romantic love. If the movies we watch are any guide, we are confident that romantic love can overcome any difficulty.[2] Consider, if you will, a few films made in the past two decades. In *Notting Hill,* Hugh Grant plays the frumpy but adorable travelogue bookstore owner who falls in love with the movie star played by Julia Roberts. Julia Roberts, in turn, plays the heart-of-gold prostitute in *Pretty Woman* who, we know, wins the heart of the ruthless financier played by Richard Gere. In the closing scene, Julia and Richard ride off in his limo into the sunset. In *Titanic*, a working-class American youth (Leonardo DiCaprio) falls in love with a wealthy debutante (Kate Winslet). In *Kate and Leopold*, the driven marketing executive (Meg Ryan) falls for the English duke (Hugh Jackman), who has traveled through time into the present, his chivalrous demeanor still in tact. These films rely on the improbable to bring two people together from dramatically different worlds and value systems and then celebrate an inexplicable faith that romance and romance alone is enough to triumph over the real and obvious differences between the two parties involved.

By contrast, the death knell of many an onscreen relationship is the appearance of mere contentment and comfort in the company of another. Meg Ryan can try all she wants to convince herself that her relationship with her fiancé (Bill Pullman) is on solid ground in the film, *Sleepless in Seattle*, but we know that mere contentment will be no match for the romantic imaginings associated with her long-anticipated meeting with the character played by Tom Hanks. Here is a film about romance where the couple only meets at the end of the film—a meeting, I should point out, fated to take place on the observation deck of the Empire State building, reenacting the famous meeting of Cary Grant and Deborah Kerr in *An Affair to Remember*. Everything about the "relationship" prior to that scene was based on romantic fantasy and what little was revealed during a call-in talk radio show.

In another Ryan/Hanks film, *You've Got Mail*, Ryan, owner of a small children's bookstore, is in a contented relationship with Greg Kinear, a local columnist. Early scenes of their relationship offer lively conversation, a genuine respect for each other, and a shared set of values and common vision of the world in which they live. But there is no evident romance between them. Yet when she finally (after a lengthy e-mail–only relationship) meets the character played by Tom Hanks, a person whose crassly consumerist approach to selling books she despises, we sense immediately that there is a romantic tension between them that will soon be the center of the film and triumph over such petty matters as common values, vision, and intellectually stimulating conversation.

We should also note the close relationship between romance and sexual passion in Hollywood films. It is a cinematic commonplace in many romantic movies to include a sequence in which a couple's blossoming relationship is depicted through a montage of scenes, usually accompanied by some lush musical theme song, showing the couple walking hand in hand on the beach, playfully splashing each other in a park fountain, and making love with wild abandon between the sheets. These scenes demonstrate that each has found what he or she was looking for in the other.

Imagine an altogether different montage. Scene one shows a couple herding children into the back of a minivan; scene two shows a woman paying bills at the kitchen table while the man washes dishes; scene three reveals a woman hauling in groceries from the car, while scene four shows a man trying to give cough syrup to a screaming three-year-old. In the final scene we see the couple, finally relaxing in bed, reading together. Soon they turn to kiss each other, turn out the light, and go to sleep. Not even Julia Roberts and Richard Gere could turn this montage into a hymn to romance. And yet, for most married couples, this second montage is far closer to their experience.

We are schooled by advertising, television, and film to evaluate love relationships on their capacity to deliver the thrill of romance and the promise of passion. Glamour magazines counsel readers on how to "keep the romance alive" in their love relationships. In a likely reaction to a premodern world in which marriages were arranged and wives were treated as chattel in an economic merger between two families, we have now arrived at the place in which romantic love becomes, as Niklas Luhmann has observed, "the sole legitimate reason for the choice of a partner."[3] The relationship is considered an end in itself. So our culture suggests that the decisive criterion for the health of a marriage lies in the ability to sustain romance, that is, to have long intimate conversations together, candlelight dinners for two, passionate and frequent sex.

How can any ordinary marriage hope to live up to such unrealistic expectations? Any compelling spirituality of marriage must explore an account of ordinary human relationships, the value of which cannot be measured by the hopelessly unrealistic standards of romance and passion that dominate our cultural landscape.

The Myth of "The Right One"

Closely related to our modern preoccupation with romance is the cultural myth, fueled again by Hollywood and television, that somewhere out there is the perfect partner for us. We choose our future mate out of the conviction that he or she is that "right person," the one who was "meant for me." The myth of "the right one" is often articulated in the language of "soul mates." The National Marriage Project, associated with Rutgers University, in its report, *The State of Our Unions—2001*, studied the attitudes of those in their twenties about marriage today and about their choice of future life partners. According to the study, "the overwhelming majority (94 percent) of never-married singles agree that 'when you marry you want your spouse to be your soul mate, first and foremost.'" Almost as large a majority (88 percent) agree that "there is a special person, a soul mate, waiting for you somewhere out there." The authors of the study express concern that "the centuries-old ideal of friendship in marriage, or what sociologists call *companionate marriage*, may be evolving into a more exalted and demanding standard of a spiritualized union of souls." It is a not altogether surprising reaction to the divorce culture in which these young people have been raised, but, the authors fear, "the soul mate ideal of marriage may create unrealistic expectations that, if unfulfilled, may lead to marital discontent and perhaps search for a new soul mate."[4]

The popular romantic assumption that there is *"one right person out there waiting for me"* is often underwritten in popular Christian spirituality. Many Christians speak of God's plan under the assumption that this divine "plan" includes God's choice of mate for them. The spiritual dilemma, of course, is that God does not reveal the name to us. The task of the single Christian, we think, is to somehow discern God's plan in order to determine who it was that God had chosen for them. "The right one" has now become a part of divine providence, which means that, again, if a given marital relationship fails to live up to expectations, it will not be hard to convince myself that I simply failed to listen to God when I made the original choice of spouse. An adequate spirituality of marriage requires, I believe, an alternative understanding of divine providence.

Consumer Culture

The power of romance discussed previously takes a very particular shape within a consumer society. By *consumer society,* I mean a society in which the logic of consumer choice and product comparison becomes the default logic by which we make virtually all of our significant life choices. We live in a society driven by a free-market economy. That economy thrives when we act as consumers. We must continue to purchase goods and services if we are to "grow the economy." To some extent, we act as consumers out of genuine need, as when we purchase shelter, clothing, and food for ourselves and our family. However, this kind of subsistence purchasing provides a very tenuous foundation for an economy. Consequently, if the economy is to grow, a marketing industry is required to manipulate people's desire for goods and services. The economy's survival depends on the ability of marketing agencies to convince us that our life is horribly deficient without product X. In a free-market economy desire is, by necessity, nomadic. In other words, desire must be manipulated in such a way that no sooner do I purchase product X then my attention will be redirected toward the need for product Y. A simple example may help.

I own a cell phone that is quite serviceable; it allows me to communicate with my friends and family. As such, this cell phone will serve me quite well for several years. However, the cell phone companies can hardly grow if I am content to own the same cell phone for two years. Consequently, they must redirect my desire for a cell phone from my current one to a new model. They now offer me the promise of a slimmer model that can provide more services—it can take digital photos and connect me to the Internet. My desire now shifts from a device that allows me to communicate with others to a device that offers me other services as well. My desire is no longer satisfied by my older cell phone.

There are limits to the extent to which an industry can provide better, more useful products. Enter yet another feature of our consumer culture: fashion and style. Vincent Miller has observed that "advertising encourages consumption by increasing desire for different and newer products; style provides a way of shortening the useful life of products without diminishing quality."[5] What has resulted, he contends, is an altogether new reality, imaginary consumption. Advertising elicits a desire not for the product itself, but for the image of the product, its status or *cachet*. The actual usefulness or function of a product is eclipsed by its image and appearance. Thinking of a well-known retail chain for women's lingerie, Miller has wryly observed that perhaps this is "Victoria's real secret"![6]

Miller contends that the dynamisms of our consumer culture run deeper than we might imagine. Consumerism shapes not only our obvious choices regarding the products we purchase, but our approach to leisure, religion, and even our life partners.[7] Listen carefully to engaged couples discussing their choice of their partner and you will hear the logic of the marketplace and product comparison: "unlike my previous boyfriends, Jason really listened to me when I talked about my work." "Sally was the first woman I dated who had all the qualities I was looking for in a wife." Should it surprise us then if Jason and Sally will ultimately be set aside when, ten years down the road, their partners discover a shiny, slimmer model with dazzling new options? Such is the logic of a consumer culture.

Our consumer society is also driven by the maximization of choice. If cable television offers access to fifty channels but a satellite dish can transmit more than a hundred different viewing choices, we see it as almost self-evident that, all things being equal, we would prefer the satellite's expanded offerings. If the corner grocery offered us all of the basic food staples necessary to meet our nutritional needs in a context that allowed for familiarity with our grocer and regular interaction with our neighbors, it still could not compete with the latest supermarket's dramatically expanded grocery offerings. If modern cultural patterns are any indication, Americans generally opt for the maximization of choice over the intangible benefits of shopping at a corner grocery.

Alongside this consumerist obsession with expanding the range of choices available to us is our growing preoccupation with technological disburdenment.[8] Modern technology offers us the goods we desire without the effort that had once been necessary to procure those goods. Consider our changing relationship to music. If we had lived in 1907 rather than 2007, a love for music would normally have led us to take up the discipline of making music either through singing or playing a musical instrument. Today the modern recording industry has made music ubiquitous; we hear it in the doctor's waiting room, when we are put on hold on the telephone, in our cars on our daily work commute, or anywhere we wish if we carry with us an MP3 player. We can even receive unlimited radio channels in the most remote locations through the use of a miniature satellite device. The precious good of music acquired only by discipline and effort has now become a carefully packaged commodity. The microwave oven offers a nominally nourishing meal without the time-consuming effort that a home-cooked meal demands. Technology offers the goods we desire without effort or burden.

We must consider the consequences for marriage of this cultural preoccupation with the maximization of choice and the view that burden and effort are realities to be technologically overcome. When we are encouraged to trade in our car every few years for a newer model, does not this mentality influence us when we experience the inevitable difficulties that commitment to any one individual entails? Is not the flourishing pornography industry but the logical consequence of the technological tendency to offer the goods we desire (in this case, the delights of sexual pleasure) purged of all of the depth, texture, and "friction" that comes with any meaningful human relationship? Christian convictions about marriage must challenge the growing cultural assumption that marriage is simply one more consumer choice.[9]

Therapy as a Paradigm for Marriage

Sociologist Robert Bellah contends that the one of the distinctive features of our modern cultural landscape is the way in which therapy has replaced friendship as a model for healthy human relationships. Tune in to any episode of Oprah's hit talk show, and you hear romantic relationships discussed in language heavily dependent on the lingo of modern therapy. People "own their feelings" and "give themselves permission to explore other possibilities." They consider whether their significant other is "meeting their needs." It should not surprise us that the most popular returning guest on Oprah, a man who eventually earned his own television show, was "Dr. Phil." My intent is not to disparage the value of psychotherapy. Doubtless many, including myself, have been helped immeasurably by therapeutic relationships. The point that Bellah wishes to make is not that therapy is bad, but that the therapeutic relationship has come to represent an unspoken standard for all authentic, intimate relationships. Why is this troubling? Whereas friendship privileges a selfless commitment to the other, the therapeutic relationship is quite different. In the therapist's office there is, first of all, a profound asymmetry in the dynamics: the client talks and the therapist listens; the client discloses while the therapist withholds. Second, in the therapeutic relationship, the client is invited to talk, without self-censorship, about oneself for an entire hour. The point of the encounter is for the client to get something for him or herself. There is no real mutuality. Because the therapist must be paid, there is an economic dimension to the relationship; that is, the value of the relationship is given a monetary evaluation.[10]

If Bellah is correct in his judgment that the therapeutic

relationship has replaced friendship as the norm for evaluating our most significant human relationships, then we should not be surprised when we hear, with alarming frequency, of marriages that have ended because one's spouse is no longer "meeting my needs" or "giving me the space to grow." Such conclusions reveal a set of expectations about marriage that simply cannot be reconciled, in my view, with a Christian account of marriage. All good marriages meet *some* of our needs *some* of the time, but no marriage can meet *all* of our needs *all* of the time and, to the extent that our culture offers us models that lead us to expect as much, we will never be able to cultivate a fruitful lifelong marriage with another.

Changing Conceptions of the Household in America

David McCarthy, a contemporary theologian, and cultural commentators such as Mary Howell and Edward Shorter, have identified a cultural shift in America over the past fifty years or so regarding how we view the American household. McCarthy describes it as a shift from an "open household" to a "closed household."[11]

The premodern family was constituted, by necessity, as an open household. According to McCarthy, an *open household* is a household with relatively permeable boundaries that is dependent on three distinct but overlapping social networks of kinfolk, friends, and neighbors. *Kinfolk* refers to those persons with whom we are usually related by blood and with whom we have lifelong commitments. *Friends* refer to those persons with whom we have relationships sustained by something less than a lifelong commitment, and *neighbors* denote those with whom we share some common geographic space. The open household is sustained by these three overlapping networks of relationships. This open household, common in premodern society, was actually sustained for a considerable period well into the modern period. Its gradual dissolution has come only in the last generation or two. The open household was not, generally speaking, sustained by functional relationships freely entered into and freely dissolved by choice. Two of these spheres of relationships were experienced as givens. To put it simply, you do not choose your family and, to some extent, you do not choose your neighbors. Within an open household the daily rhythm of family life demanded interaction with sometimes helpful, sometimes gossipy and judgmental, neighbors and relatives. The needs of the household and its members were met through this large and diffuse network of relationships. Within this network there was much less focus on the nuclear family. Child-rearing was not the sole responsibility of the father and mother, but was shared by extended family, friends, and neighbors. Economic necessity demanded the pooling of resources and the bartering of skills among these spheres of relations. In fact, one of the most important characteristics of the open household was the network of reciprocal gift exchange and mutual obligation. These relationships involved significant responsibilities and obligations (for example, to supervise neighborhood kids, to mow the yard of the ailing elderly couple across the street, to keep keys to one another's homes, to borrow tools and cooking ingredients, to watch a single mom's kids one day a week). We should not romanticize such a social arrangement. Open households placed real and often harsh limits on one's privacy and autonomy.

Over the last several generations, McCarthy and other cultural commentators have suggested that a new household ideal has emerged, one that is driven by the fear that we are losing control over our lives. The new familial goal becomes independence and autonomy.[12] Think of the young family today just starting out, often forced to live in a crowded and noisy apartment complex. Their single-minded goal is to move up to a home with sufficient space that neighbors would no longer be intrusive. It is not that they are unfriendly; they just wish to be able to choose when they will and will not interact with their neighbors. The front porch, once the social space for spontaneous interactions with passersby, is supplanted by the fenced-in backyard deck, where guests are entertained strictly by invitation. Cumbersome household responsibilities, such as landscaping, painting the house, housecleaning, and mowing the lawn, that once were engaged by extended family and neighbors (the boy down the street would mow the lawn, the next-door neighbor might shovel the elderly couple's driveway) are now professionally contracted out.[13] It is less messy this way and less awkward if the job is not done well.

An additional factor explaining this shift is our increased mobility, often required by changing economic conditions. Employees are far less likely to work for the same company throughout their career, and therefore, are far less likely to live in the same neighborhood or civic community. Diminished job security brings with it the likelihood of frequent relocation in search of work, which, in turn, makes sustaining dependable relationships with friends, family, and neighbors far more difficult.

Numerous sociological studies have noted Americans' diminished civic participation. This shift was explored in the book, *Bowling Alone,* by Harvard sociologist Robert Putnam.[14] In that volume, Putnam used the leisure activity of bowling as a metaphor for changing American social patterns. Bowling, he notes, is America's most popular competitive sport, even if it is a sport that seems more suggestive of a lifestyle from decades past. In fact, more Americans are bowling today than ever before. Yet, participation in bowling *leagues* has plummeted. Americans are more likely than ever today to "bowl alone." Putnam sees this apparently trivial shift in leisure pattern as a metaphor for a larger cultural transformation. Americans are less inclined to engage in civic activities, for leisure or philanthropic purposes, that bring them into regular engagement with others. This pattern of diminished social engagements with others means that Americans have less *social capital* on which to draw. By *social capital* he means that set of social relationships on which people rely for support. The more a person is invested in a network of meaningful relationships with others, the more one can draw on one's social "bank" during times of need for support or assistance.

Putnam's observations are echoed in a recent Duke University study that documents a very disturbing trend; whereas in 1985 Americans reported having, on the average, three close friends, now they report having only two. Moreover, 25 percent of the population now report that they have no one with whom to discuss matters of personal significance.[15] Americans are socializing less and less with others outside their immediate household, and they have fewer and fewer friends on whom they can rely.

This shift from an open to a closed household and Americans' diminished social capital have had momentous consequences for the institution of marriage today. The result is a more introverted understanding of marriage wherein the couple is expected to meet all of each other's needs because that larger web of human relationships characteristic of the open household is no longer available. When things begin to go wrong in the relationship, as they eventually will, there is often no one for the couple to turn to for support.

Any adequate spirituality of marriage must take into account this shift from the open to the closed household. Many factors that led to this shift are likely to be permanent features within our culture. It is difficult to imagine that our society will gravitate back to the open household of the premodern era. We may wish to explore, however, whether opportunities exist in this new cultural situation for Christian communities to fill the breach left by modern households' lessened reliance on extended family, friends, and neighbors.

All five characteristics of contemporary North American culture that we have explored have had a profound impact on married life today. In this book, I make a sustained argument for a spirituality of Christian marriage that can confront some of these forces, forces that have helped create a veritable culture of divorce. This does not mean that divorce is never an appropriate option for couples today. Human weakness, poor choices, the unwillingness of a marriage partner to keep his or her commitment, the threat of physical or psychological harm—these and other factors may lead one to make a defensible choice to permanently end a marital relationship. I am not saying that divorce is always wrong, but rather that too many marital relationships unnecessarily end in divorce. Too often the cultural forces just discussed have tragically led many couples to conclude that there was something fatally wrong in their relationship, something that could not be remedied, when in fact theirs was a commitment that, grounded in an adequate spirituality, could have been healthy and fruitful.

This brief reflection on the shape of North American culture leads to a reflection on the Christian tradition in the next chapter. How might some of Christianity's central faith convictions help generate a spirituality of marriage capable of responding to the cultural characteristics that we have just considered?

Questions for Reflection and Discussion

1. A central claim of this chapter is that the consumerism rampant in our culture is so widespread that it affects our choices about the religion we practice, the church we attend, and even our choice of life partner. What other examples of this consumerist mentality have you encountered?

2. In what ways does your own experience support or contradict Putnam and the Duke University's study on Americans' diminished *social capital?* To what extent have you witnessed in your own life a diminished involvement in regular social activities with others?

3. What are some ways in our personal relationships in which we can find a balance between "meeting our needs" and honoring the Christian call to place ourselves at the service of others?

Chapter Two

MARRIAGE AND FAITH

Spirituality is a relatively modern term. At one time it suggested a kind of piety. Today it often refers to the "otherworldly," the mystical or paranormal. I will use the word *spirituality* to refer to the particular shape and texture of our encounter with God in our daily lives. Any authentic spirituality, by revealing to us God's action in our lives, also discloses our truest identity; we "find" ourselves in our relationships with God and one another. A spirituality of marriage, then, is concerned with the distinct manner in which God's transforming presence and action are encountered in our marriages. A *marital spirituality* should help us discover the ways in which, through our fidelity to the spiritual discipline of faithful marital living, we discover our truest identity before God.

As Christians, our particular faith convictions should play an essential role in our spiritual life in general and in our marriages in particular. In my background reading in preparation for this book, I was impressed with the way authors who wrote on the spirituality of marriage so gracefully and effectively wove the insights of contemporary psychology and counseling into their reflections. This approach has been of enormous help for many married couples who have looked to these books for concrete guidance. However, I was less impressed with the attempts to integrate basic faith commitments into marital spirituality. Understandably, the authors wished to avoid heavy-handed dogmatic treatments or intellectual flights into the stratosphere. However, I think it is a mistake to assume that the content of our faith has no positive role to play in developing a marital spirituality.

Throughout this book, as I reflect on marital spirituality, I will draw on four basic faith convictions that I believe contribute much to a spirituality of marriage:

1. All humans, deep within their hearts, long for relationship with God.
2. In Jesus, God reveals to us what it means to be truly and fully human.
3. In Jesus' life, death, and resurrection we discover the distinctive pattern or rhythm of Christian living.
4. To believe that God is triune is to believe that God, at the core of the divine being, is perfect loving relationship.

I hope to demonstrate that these basic faith convictions are not just doctrinal abstractions but provide concrete material for reflection on the spiritual dimension of our marriages.

Our Longing for God

I have a good friend who experienced a difficult bout with depression over several months. She shared with me that at times she found it difficult just to get out of bed in the morning. Yet she did, if only because she knew that getting out of bed in the morning is what we do when we are healthy, and though she knew she was not healthy, she felt that the only thing that prevented her from taking her own life was acting as if she were.

Why do healthy people get out of bed each morning and face the world? I believe that at some deep center of our being we expect something from the day or, at the very least, we *long for* something from the day. Within each of us is an inner restlessness, an insufficiency that impels us to engage our world, to forge meaningful relationships with others, to exercise our imaginations. The vitality of a human life can be measured by the intensity of one's desire. We know we are truly alive when we experience a drive for the "more" of life. Human desire or longing is the source of our spiritual energy. It is what impels us in our most creative labors and moves us to enter into relationship with others. It is encountered when a man aches for the woman he loves, when a software designer pushes herself to perfect a product she is creating, when a mother longs for an absent child, when a lawyer defends the defenseless in search of justice, when a bereaved soul yearns to have others know his pain and loss.

It is bedrock biblical wisdom that the human person was not created for isolation; the way of the hermit has always been the cautious exception rather than the rule in the Christian tradition. No, we are made for communion, driven into relationship by a deep sense that by connecting with another we might find wholeness and be sated. For a time we may even experience something of this wholeness. But it does not, and indeed cannot, last. The desires that well up within us cannot be definitively satisfied by anything in our world. In a well-known passage, Saint Augustine wrote in his *Confessions*, "Our hearts are restless, Lord, until they rest in you."[1] Perhaps no Christian writer so perceptively grasped the spiritual power of desire as the twelfth-century Cistercian monk Bernard of Clairvaux. For Bernard, "desire is the form love takes in our earthly existence."[2] This sense of human longing for relationship is not rooted in some animal need for mating and the survival of the species. Bernard believed that the source of human desire was the image and likeness of God inscribed in our very being. The longing for the communion we experience with another wells up from our longing for God and offers us a real yet imperfect participation in the holy mystery that alone can completely fulfill us.

Human desire, quite obviously, is important for an understanding of marriage. After all, without the desire to love and be loved by another, no one would ever enter into a relationship as demanding as marriage. This is why marriages are most at risk during those periods when one or both spouses experience a waning of desire. I am not primarily speaking of sexual desire but of

that basic desire for communion with another and the way of life
that real communion offers. Any authentic marital spirituality
must attend to this human experience of desire and the drive for
meaningful relationship with another.

Jesus Reveals to Us Our Humanity

In the early 1960s, Catholic bishops from all around the world
gathered at the Second Vatican Council. This event brought about
the most significant reform and renewal of Catholicism in four
centuries. One of the most remarkable documents produced by
the council was The Pastoral Constitution on the Church in the
Modern World *(Gaudium et Spes)*. In this document the bishops
called on the Church to look at the world not just as an enemy
to be conquered but as a dialogue partner. The Church must try
to understand the problems and challenges facing humanity today. The bishops believed that Christianity can offer a meaningful response. Christianity offers the world Jesus Christ, not as
some otherworldly being foreign to human experience, but as the
fulfillment of all we were created to be. They wrote:

> In reality it is only in the mystery of the Word made flesh
> that the mystery of man truly becomes clear....Christ the
> new Adam, in the very revelation of the mystery of the
> Father and of his love, fully reveals man to himself and
> brings to light his most high calling.[3]

We refer to this as the mystery of the *incarnation*, the belief that
in Jesus of Nazareth, God is encountered not simply through imperfect intermediaries but in an unprecedented closeness. In Jesus,
God has definitively taken our human reality as God's own. Jesus
is the human face of God's love for us.

And yet our sense of Jesus has been distorted by the fact that
the four gospels in the New Testament do not offer detailed biogra-
phies of Jesus' life but theologically interpreted, selective accounts
of, for the most part, only his public ministry. Consequently, when

we think of Jesus, we recall his dynamic preaching and spellbinding stories, walking on water, changing water into wine, raising Lazarus from the dead, healing the blind and the lame, and exorcising demons. He is for us the Son of God whom we worship. That is all well and good, but it rather empties the significance of saying, as does the Letter to the Hebrews, that Jesus was like us in all things but sin. A person who raises the dead and walks on water does not look that much like us at all!

This brings us to an often overlooked question. The Bible reports to us the dramatic circumstances surrounding Jesus' birth, the many signs and wonders that Jesus performed much later in life, the great teachings he left us, and the redemptive power of his suffering, death, and resurrection. But what of the thirty or so years of Jesus' life between his birth and his public ministry? We know very little of the life of Jesus during this time, but we can surmise a few likely facts and these are worthy of reflection.

First, Jesus was a layperson. It may seem odd to put the matter that way, but it is an important point. The tendency to think of Jesus in priestly terms has been no doubt encouraged by the subsequent Catholic theological tradition that spoke of the ordained priest of the Church acting as "another Christ" or functioning "in the person of Christ, the head of the Church." Yet there is no biblical evidence that Jesus was of either Levitical or priestly descent. Even in his public ministry he acted always as a Jewish layperson. There is but one book of the New Testament, the Letter to the Hebrews, that refers to Jesus as our high priest. Nowhere else in the New Testament is priestly language ever applied to Jesus. If Jesus was a Jewish layman, then he could not rely on any official authority—his authority was an authority of character, not of office. This means that, at least prior to his public ministry, his life would not have been any different from the life of any other Jewish male.

And what of Jesus' marital status? This question is an old one, but it has been given new life thanks to Dan Brown's novel and the subsequent film, *The Da Vinci Code,* which speculated on a possible marriage between Jesus and Mary Magdalene. The

New Testament is completely silent on this matter. However, in light of the frequent mention of other key figures having wives or having left their wives to follow Jesus, it is unlikely that a wife of Jesus would go without note. But what can we infer from this? The fact that Jesus was probably not married itself tells us little. Apart from one brief passage that speaks of those who make themselves *"eunuchs for the sake of the kingdom of heaven"* (Matthew 19:12), there is little to suggest whether Jesus' celibacy had any religious significance. It was very common for women to marry young, often in their early teens. But this was not necessarily the case for men, who frequently married much later in life.

Being single is one thing; being a consecrated celibate—choosing lifelong celibacy as an expression of one's religious commitment—is something else altogether. Even if Jesus never married, there is little evidence that he considered himself a formal, consecrated celibate (in the tradition, for example, of the Jewish Essene community, which set celibacy as a precondition for membership in their monastic community), at least prior to his public ministry. Although the matter cannot be pursued here, this simple fact about Jesus might yield great fruit for a spirituality of the single person. It suggests that in Jesus we discover a person who was neither married nor a consecrated celibate and yet found human fulfillment in free and intimate relationships with friends of both sexes.

Mark 6:3 tells us that Jesus was a carpenter—a woodworker, that is, a basic craftsman who would have built rudimentary furniture, plows, or yokes. As such he would have been a step or two above a slave or day laborer in socioeconomic class.[4] In any event, we know that Jesus practiced a trade.

We do know that aside from his practicing a trade, Jesus presumably took care of a family. Indirect biblical evidence leads us to conclude that Joseph had died before Jesus began his public ministry. The frequent references to Mary and his "brothers and sisters"[5] suggest that whatever precise relations bound him to these "brothers and sisters" they saw themselves as "family" who felt that it was within their rights to lay claim to his attention (see Mark 3:31–35).

To put the matter straightforwardly, by all appearances Jesus lived a fairly ordinary and unexceptional life before his brief public ministry. He practiced a trade and attended to his family obligations to his mother and other kin. We have no record of his performing great miracles during this time. There is no indication of any adolescent "sermons on the mount." What is the significance of this? It suggests that when God chose to embrace humanity in this unique fashion almost two thousand years ago, he embraced *our* world, a world filled with mundane daily tasks for which few are canonized: the world of family and work, the world of simple meals, simple homes, and simple pleasures. He took all that is ordinary and, to our modern eyes, boring and without value, and he blessed it, thereby manifesting its holiness.

Our belief in the incarnation is, among other things, a belief in the intrinsic sacredness of the most basic of human activities and relationships: work, leisure, and family. This suggests that a spirituality of marriage needs to find God not only in church or on one's knees in prayer, but in shared labor, shared leisure, and in the characteristic practices and commitments necessary for nurturing a shared household.

Life-Death-Life Is the Paradoxical Logic of Human Fulfillment

For many Christians, belief in the saving work of Christ begins and ends with the passion, death, resurrection, and ascension of Christ, sometimes called the *paschal mystery*. The term *paschal* recalls the Hebrew Passover (Pasch), in which God delivered the Israelites from slavery into freedom. Christians hold that in death Christ too "passed over" into the Father, effecting our own liberation from sin. Many Christian traditions hold that the celebration of the sacraments, particularly through baptism and the Eucharist, is a means of ritually uniting ourselves with Christ in this paschal mystery. But it is a mistake to think of the paschal mystery only in connection with the final events of Jesus' life. For what transpired in the last days of Jesus' life on earth was but a dramatic culmination of his entire life. The central challenge of Christian life is to internalize and make this spiritual rhythm of life-death-life our own. With Jesus we are to *live* out of the assurance that we are God's good creatures, *die* to any tendency to make ourselves the ultimate reality in the universe, and *live* anew in lives of loving attentiveness and service to others. What Jesus lived, he also taught: *"Unless a grain of wheat falls into the earth and dies, it remains just a single grain; but if it dies, it bears much fruit"* (John 12:24). In his life and in his teaching, Jesus offered us a new vision of human wholeness in which *death* and *life* are infused with new meaning. In this vein, Ronald Rolheiser distinguishes between two kinds of death and two kinds of life:

> First, regarding two kinds of death: there is *terminal* death and there is *paschal* death. Terminal death is a death that ends life and ends possibilities. Paschal death, like terminal death, is real. However, paschal death is a death that, while ending one kind of life, opens the person undergoing it to receive a deeper and richer form of life. The image of the grain of wheat falling into the ground and dying so as to produce new life is an image of paschal death. There are also two kinds of life: there is *resuscitated* life and there is *resurrected* life. Resuscitated life is when one is restored to one's former life and health, as is the case with someone who has been clinically dead and is brought back to life. Resurrected life is not this. It is not a restoration of one's old life but the reception of a radically new life.[6]

We are thus introduced to the peculiar program for Christian living. If you want to be happy, seek the happiness of others. If you would be fulfilled, abandon the quest for fulfillment. To delight in the gifts of creation, you must learn on occasion to abstain from them. To know the joy of the feast, you must embrace the longing that arises from the fast.

For the martyrs of the early Church, their witness to the power of the paschal mystery took the most dramatic form imaginable:

it was through the free offering of their very lives that they gave eloquent and sometimes shocking testimony to the power of the cross and resurrection. The witness of the early martyrs eventually gave way to the asceticism of monastic and consecrated religious life. Those who publicly committed themselves to poverty, chastity, obedience, and sometimes stability (the commitment to live the balance of one's life in one religious house), were freely embracing the limits these vows imposed on them in order to more profoundly enter into the paschal pattern of life-death-life. The Church still benefits greatly from the evangelical witness of those who embrace the paschal mystery in such a public way through their vows. Yet the time has come to acknowledge that the way of Christian asceticism so often associated with the "vowed life" is not limited to consecrated religious men and women. Authentic Christian marriage is also a form of public "vowed life."

Christian marriage has been shrouded in ambiguity and suspicion from the very beginning of Christianity. It was not universally recognized as a sacrament until the thirteenth century. Most Protestant traditions, although valuing marriage as an important dimension of Christian life, do not consider it a sacrament today. Significant disagreements over when a marriage was considered indissoluble and other such questions obscured its evangelical value. In marriage, two people exchange vows, freely entering into a permanent covenantal relationship with each other. As with consecrated religious life, the heart of this commitment, its spiritual core, is the freely accepted decision to embrace the limits that these vows impose. This means that marriage is every bit as much a paschal or ascetical vocation as that of the monk, vowed religious, nun, or priest. As seen in the next two chapters, marriage, too, involves the free embrace of limits as an opportunity to enter into the paschal mystery.

The Book of Genesis reminds us that we are created in the image and likeness of God (see Genesis 1:26–27). It is a way of saying that there is something vital within us that allows us to share or participate in God's life. When we are authentically human and give ourselves over to our deepest longing for human communion, we are, at the same time, participating in the divine. This idea of participation in the life of God has been affirmed in many different ways by some of the greatest voices in the Christian tradition. Yet its implications for spirituality have often been overlooked. To understand it we must turn to one of the most fundamental and yet misunderstood doctrines in our tradition, the Trinity.

The Trinity

Most Christians believe in the doctrine of the Trinity, that basic Christian teaching that God exists as three divine persons sharing in one divine nature. Yet because, on the face of it, this claim makes no sense (how can 3 = 1?), their belief fails to challenge the conventional ways in which they imagine God.

What is this conventional way of imagining God? Most of us think of God as an individual superbeing. As such, we believe that God is infinitely more powerful than ourselves, all-knowing, all-loving, but just another being, nonetheless. We use Trinitarian language—Father, Son, and Spirit—but in ways that suggest God is, if not a divine individual, a kind of divine consortium: "two men and a bird," as some have put it. Both viewpoints actually cash out in much the same way. Whether God is conceived as a single super-being or as a divine consortium—in either case, God is another individual being or set of beings to whom I must relate along with the other claims on my attention.

This way of imagining God has had a pervasive and almost completely negative impact on Christian spirituality because it places God in competition with our other, more worldly concerns. This image of God as a superbeing, a kind of Christian "Zeus," leads us to see our life as an endless tug of war between the matters that demand our attention in the daily course of human affairs—preparing classes, buying groceries, playing with our children, talking with our spouses—and our religious obligations to God. Years ago the great Jesuit scientist and mystic, Teilhard de Chardin, captured the consequences of such a way of imagining God:

I do not think I am exaggerating when I say that nine out of ten practicing Christians feel that [human] work is always at the level of a "spiritual encumbrance." In spite of the practice of right intentions, and the day offered every morning to God, the general run of the faithful dimly feel that time spent at the office or the studio, in the fields or in the factory, is time taken away from prayer and adoration. It is impossible not to work—that is taken for granted. Then it is impossible, too, to aim at the deep religious life reserved for those who have the leisure to pray or preach all day long. A few moments of the day can be salvaged for God, yes, but the best hours are absorbed, or at any rate, cheapened, by material cares. Under the sway of this feeling, large numbers of Catholics lead a double or crippled life in practice.[7]

Such a perspective cannot help but have an impact on our view of the Christian vocation to marriage and family. My commitment to my spouse and children, as well as to my career, becomes a distraction that immediately relegates me to second-class citizenship in the kingdom of God. This image of God has led many to assume, wrongly, that a spirituality of marriage must be concerned with sacralizing my marriage by desperately inserting as many religious moments into our day—snatches of time for Scripture reading or private devotions, early-morning daily Mass, grace at meals, and so on—that become our only hope for preserving some frail contact with a God to whom we do not have the luxury of "praying without ceasing."

Regrettably, in the Catholic tradition there are distorted theologies of committed celibacy that assume this perspective and suggest that the committed celibate, free from the "distractions" of marriage and family, is better able to love God.[8] From this came a spirituality of "detachment" in which it was thought that spiritual growth meant detaching oneself from anything that distracted one from God. When the great Trappist monk and spiritual writer Thomas Merton wrote of the spirituality of detachment, he felt compelled to clarify that detachment did not mean a detachment from things in themselves:

> Detachment from things does not mean setting up a con-
> tradiction between "things" and "God" as if God were
> another "thing" and as if His creatures were His rivals.
> We do not detach ourselves from things in order to attach
> ourselves to God, but rather we become detached *from
> ourselves* in order to see and use all things in and for God.
> This is an entirely new perspective which many sincerely
> moral and ascetic minds fail utterly to see. There is no
> evil in anything created by God, nor can anything of His
> become an obstacle to our union with Him. The obstacle
> is in our "self," that is to say in the tenacious need to
> maintain our separate, external, egotistical will.[9]

Were this image of God as a remote superbeing our only available way of imagining God, there would not be any point in ex-
ploring a spirituality of marriage; the only realistic approach to
marital spirituality within this framework would be the simple
injunction: pray more! To counter this all-too-common imaginative framework we must recover the deeper insights from our
Christian tradition embedded in the doctrine of the Trinity.

Our belief that God is triune means that God is not to be
imagined as an individual superbeing or set of "persons" that exists alongside all other beings in the cosmos. Rather, the doctrine
of the Trinity teaches us that God is best imagined as the divine
source and superabundant dynamism of love, not an individual but
a divine movement, not an object but the very spiritual atmosphere
of our lives. In the early Church the formal doctrinal language
of the Trinity emerged out of a basic experience of God. Early
Christians experienced Jesus as the concrete expression of God's
love, and the Holy Spirit as both the divine atmosphere in which
they encountered Christ and the divine power by which they were
brought into communion with God in union with Christ.

Emerging Trinitarian doctrine named the *shape* of the

Christian encounter with God. God was not a distant entity send-
ing divine intermediaries. Rather, Christians experienced God as
the divine source and superabundance of love poured forth in Jesus,
made effective by the Holy Spirit, and at every moment inviting the
believer into transformative relationship. Imagining the triune life
of God as a divine movement toward us in love points toward the
essential insight of Trinitarian doctrine: God's very being, what it
is for God *to be*, is loving, life-giving relationship. God does not
just *have* a love relationship with us, God *is* loving relationship.
This means that an imaginative view of God's relationship to us
must resist positing God as an individual being whose grace must
be imported into our world. God is that holy mystery that bears
the world up in its very existence. God is "Being-as-Communion."[10]
There is no self-contained, divine individual residing in heaven far
away from us; there is simply a dynamic movement of love that
is God, "in whom we live and move and have our being." This
framework has strong biblical roots. Saint Paul writes:

> *God's love has been poured into our hearts through the*
> *Holy Spirit that has been given to us.*
>   *For while we were still weak, at the right time Christ*
> *died for the ungodly. Indeed, rarely will anyone die for*
> *a righteous person—though perhaps for a good person*
> *someone might actually dare to die. But God proves his*
> *love for us in that while we still were sinners Christ died*
> *for us* (Romans 5:5–8).

The Johannine literature also presents God, not as an individual being whose many attributes (for example, kindness, mercy,
generosity) include "loving," but as love abiding:

> *Beloved, let us love one another, because love is from*
> *God; everyone who loves is born of God and knows God.*
> *Whoever does not love does not know God, for God is*
> *love....No one has ever seen God; if we love one another,*
> *God lives in us, and his love is perfected in us....*

> *God is love, and those who abide in love abide in*
> *God, and God abides in them....Those who say, "I love*
> *God," and hate their brothers or sisters, are liars; for*
> *those who do not love a brother or sister whom they*
> *have seen, cannot love God whom they have not seen.*
> *The commandment we have from him is this: those who*
> *love God must love their brothers and sisters also* (1 John
> 4:7–8, 12, 16, 20–21).

What we have is a biblical tradition alive to the way in which love does not just describe an attribute of God but names the essential *way* in which God is God. This view of God as fundamentally relational and engaged in our world has been expressed in the insights of the many giants of our tradition. Saint Augustine captured something of it when he spoke of God as "closer to us than we are to ourselves." Saint Thomas Aquinas assumed this perspective in his presentation of creation, not as an event in the distant past but as the ongoing relationship God has with the world. God is Creator because, even now, God is sustaining all that is, bearing the world up in divine love.

As Christianity developed a more precise Trinitarian language, it came to describe the shape of God's dynamic movement toward us in the language of *God, Word,* and *Spirit* or, alternatively, *Father, Son,* and *Spirit.* These terms should not be construed, however, as the proper names of God. God cannot be "named" in the sense that a name explains someone or something. Recall God's refusal to reveal to Moses the divine name. Unlike the other gods of antiquity, Israel's God was utterly sovereign, not to be manipulated by the controlling power of "naming." This God is disclosed to Israel in divine action, covenantal love. As Christians we should not imagine that God has given to us what God withheld from Moses. God is the mysterious "more" ever beyond us, yet always abiding with us. God discloses God's self as holy mystery, not a riddle to be solved but an inexhaustible source and realization of love to be embraced.

The God of the Covenant, the God of superabundant love,

eternally "speaks," or expresses, divine love as Word and makes that Word fertile and effective by the power of the Spirit. The Trinity outlines the shape of this eternal divine "speaking." It may be helpful to consider the root meaning of the Hebrew word for "spirit," *ruah*, which literally means "breath." When I speak a word to another, I attempt to communicate something of myself to that person. Yet that spoken word is conveyed to the other by means of my breath. Of course, the recipient of my word does not focus on my breath but rather on the word that my breath vocalizes. In like manner, we might say that in God (the Father) love is uttered as an eternal Word (the Son), and borne by the holy breath of God (the Holy Spirit) we call Spirit. As triune, God who is love eternally offers God's self as love spoken and love made effective. Michael Downey describes the felt experience of this Christian conviction regarding the nature of God:

> While the teaching about the Trinity...may be dismissed as a vexing puzzle by many, in the ordinary lives of the Christian faithful there is indeed some grasp of the mystery which the doctrine seeks to express. In other words, there is often a deep experience of the Father as the originator and Pure Source of Love, Jesus Christ the Son who is that Love seen and heard in Word, and the Spirit as the ongoing and inexhaustible activity of that Love, drawing everything and everyone back to the origin and end of Love in the bonding of Love itself.[11]

The deep wisdom of Christian intuitions about the being of God lies in the Trinitarian affirmation that God is not a self-contained, distant, introverted God, but dynamic, personal, relational, fecund, and inclusive of all reality.

The spiritual challenge of our lives lies not in desperately setting aside moments for God alongside the other activities and commitments of our lives, but rather that of discovering *within* our basic human activities and commitments the possibility for communion with God in our relationships with others and, particularly, with our spouse. If God is love, if God is gift given eternally, then our participation in the life of God happens not by escaping our everyday world, but by entering more deeply into the life of love and that paradoxical logic of gift in that we receive most richly only when we make "gifting" others a way of life.

In conventional Christian piety, prayer names "religious" moments and actions in our lives. The task of the spiritual life was to accumulate as many of these as possible. The perspective I offer here is one in which prayer names those moments and activities when we consciously cultivate an awareness of the God who abides with us throughout the day. As for Christian marriage, it offers us true communion with God when, and only when, our spousal relations are drawn into the pattern of divine love and the logic of divine gift revealed to us in Trinitarian doctrine.

These first two chapters have been an extended introduction to our topic. I have laid out what I believe are two very important sets of considerations for developing a marital spirituality. First, since spirituality is not, or at least should not be, an abstraction, it must be forged in conscious response to the world in which we live. We must attend to the shape of our culture and identify where this cultural shape is conducive to or supportive of the life of discipleship and communion and where it must be confronted by the life of discipleship and communion. Second, I outlined four basic Christian commitments that I believe should form the foundation for any authentic Christian spirituality. In the following chapters I hope to tease out the fruit of this dialogue between faith and culture in forging a practical spirituality for marriage.

Questions for Reflection and Discussion

1. Do you consider yourself a "spiritual" person? Do you consider yourself a "religious" person? How do you make the connection between being religious and being spiritual in your own life?

2. In what ways did you find the presentation of God as Trinity in this chapter a challenge to your conventional view of God and in what ways did you find it consoling?

Chapter Three

MARRIAGE AND THE LIFE OF COMMUNION

The last chapter considered what it means to profess faith in a triune God. The doctrine of the Trinity asserts that at the heart of God's very being is perfect loving relationship. Consequently, God does not compete for our love and attention but can be encountered in the life of love. Wherever and whenever we enter into authentic loving communion with others, God abides. This presents wonderful possibilities for a spirituality of marriage. God is not a competing third figure in our marriage; rather, God abides whenever Diana and I live in communion with each other, our children, and the world at large. This insight bears further exploration.

The Life of Communion

When a husband and wife attend to each other, not as objects for their own gratification but as subjects of infinite dignity and worth, they enter into the life of love and their communion with each other is, at the same time, communion with God. This insight is, in my view, the indispensable foundation of any marital spirituality. God is found in the "between" of the relationship of husband and wife. In the Book of Genesis, we are told *God created humankind in his image, / in the image of God he created them; / male and female* (Genesis 1:27). The Orthodox bishop and theologian, Kallistos Ware, suggests boldly that in this biblical passage:

> ...the image of God is given, not to the man alone or to the woman alone, but to the two of them together....It comes to its fulfillment only in the "between" that unites them to each other. Personhood is a mutual gift; there is no true human unless there are at least two humans in communion with each other. To say "I am made in God's image" is to affirm: "I need you in order to be myself." The divine image is in this way a "relational" image, manifested not in isolation but in community—and, above all, in the primordial bond between husband and wife that is the foundation of all other forms of social life.[1]

To be human is to need relationship with another in order to "be myself." Marriage is simply a dramatic testimony to this basic human truth. In marriage we experience communion with our spouses—not because we are each half-selves looking for a mate as our completion—but because in marriage we find ourselves in giving ourselves to another. This "shared life of communion" is a kind of theological shorthand for the diverse ways in which married couples, in the authenticity of their daily life together, abide in God *as they attend to each other in love.* God is not a third party who must regularly be called into the marriage relationship; God abides *in* the marriage relationship itself. In other words, sometimes our most profound experience of God comes, not when we are consciously focusing on God, as in times of prayer and worship, but when we lovingly turn to embrace another in love. The cultivation of an authentic marital spirituality means not just more prayer, but the fostering of marital communion. Three concrete dimensions of this experience of marital communion are mutuality, intimacy, and companionship.

Mutuality

The word *mutuality* is often used in relation to marital life, but what does it really mean? Mutuality is manifested in human relationships wherever and whenever both parties recognize and acknowledge the giftedness of the other. This is quite different from the important, yet in itself insufficient, assertion that each spouse be treated as an equal. When we cultivate mutuality in our marriage, we are learning to recognize not only the equality of each partner but also each one's unique giftedness.

Some of the most important work that must take place in a marriage relationship concerns the cultivation of mutuality. Some time ago my wife and I were able to get out for a rare "dinner date" without the kids. Most of our dinner conversations when we are alone together end up revolving around very practical questions: our calendars, our jobs, or concerns for one of our children. On this particular evening, however, we made a conscious decision to dedicate our dinner conversation exclusively to our marriage relationship. We decided to tell each other all of the ways in which we experience the other as a gift. I told Diana of my delight in her seemingly boundless energy and determination in tackling her many family projects. I told her how her playfulness often frees me to let go of my own obsession with social propriety. She, in turn, thanked me for my commitment to see that our family comes before my career and for my conscientiousness regarding the value of making joint family decisions. The dinner was an experience of authentic mutuality as we gratefully affirmed the gifts we shared with each other in our marriage.

Much of the shared communion of married life is sustained by this dynamic whereby we both receive gifts from our spouses and receive our spouses as gifts themselves. This sense of gift cannot be quantified and measured. Nothing kills a marriage like that deadly game of marital accounting where each keeps track of the "things done for the other" with the never quite spoken expectation of reciprocation. Yet how could I possibly quantify gifts my wife offers me? I am blessed when a night ending in argument is followed by a day begun anew with a kiss. I am blessed when I return home from work venting my frustrations on my wife and yet still find myself loved and accepted. I can only receive as gift the forgiveness offered again and again in response to my own pettiness and hardness of heart. These gifts cannot be quantified in view of compensation. No, the "return gift" I offer my spouse belongs not within the realm of economic calculation but that of grace and blessing.

The offering and receiving of gifts lies at the heart of two central Christian affirmations: the Trinity and the paschal mystery. The doctrine of the Trinity reveals a "gifting God" who gives out of the depths of divine love without ever being depleted. The paschal mystery gives concrete shape to this divine gift as Jesus lived a life of self-bestowal before others. Indeed, in Jesus God displayed the deep logic of gift in the most radical form possible: the offer of one's life for another.

When my spouse and I enter the logic of gift, by what we offer to and receive from each other, we both discover our truest selves in the mutuality of our relationship and enter into the realm of the divine, where we draw from and add to "the momentum of God's giving."[2]

There is an element of delight in the experience of mutuality. At times I have snuck upstairs and listened quietly as Diana read to one of our children. I savored the enthusiasm and energy that she put into reading those stories. At other times delight gives way to pure and simple pride. I recall how I felt when Diana finally received her graduate degree, for I knew well of those many late nights when I would go to bed while she stayed up studying. Surely these moments—when we find ourselves drawn out of our own world to delight in our beloved and his or her accomplishments, when we attend to our spouse not as an object but as a gift—shape us in unseen ways.

Authentic mutuality within marriage seems to exclude the hierarchical view of the marriage relationship often advocated by fundamentalist Christians. I am convinced that hierarchically structured marriages can manifest authentic marital love and a real reciprocity, that is, a sense that marriage entails binding obligations for both parties. However, it is difficult to recognize in these marriage relationships true mutuality, for if mutuality involves the acknowledgment of gifts, hierarchical notions of the marriage relationship ask one partner, the wife, to suppress some of her gifts in deference to her spouse.

I will admit that these marriages often flourish, as both spouses engage in a form of authentic marital love and respect within this traditional structure. We lived for several years next door to a devout evangelical Christian family in which the husband and wife firmly believed in the hierarchical structure of marriage as divinely sanctioned. I do not question the sanctity of their relationship nor would I deny that both exhibited a profound love and respect for each other. But I have often wondered whether part of the reason their marriage worked lay less in the divine source of this arrangement than in the natural differentiation in their personalities such that each was already inclined by personal temperament to a particular role in the marriage. She flourished in her wide-ranging domestic responsibilities as he naturally assumed the financial and disciplinary responsibilities conventionally assigned to the male of the household.

But what happens when the natural dispositions of the spouses do not follow these "divinely sanctioned" roles? What happens when the husband possesses few career aspirations and finds his greatest satisfaction in domestic life? What happens when the wife wishes to pursue a professional career requiring a considerable investment of time and energy? What happens when couples find that they function best when all significant family decisions are made jointly rather than by one or the other functioning as head? Are such couples to be viewed as a spiritual aberration?

There are certainly times when I envy our former neighbors. When we both worked full time, Diana and I had to get up each morning and, in a sense, reinvent our relationship. We had to decide who was to pick up the kids and take them to baseball practice. We had to negotiate who would take time off from work to bring a child to a doctor's appointment. These decisions were by no means free of conflict, and at times the process was downright wearying. Our life together would doubtless have been easier if we had entered into some clear contractual agreements on our wedding day (although I suspect that more men than women would agree with me on this): "You will have all responsibilities for the kids' health and education; I will provide financial security for our family." But I also believe that such a contractual arrangement, particularly if it was made under the shadow of some vague divine sanction (for example, "this is what Christian wives are supposed to do"), brings with it serious risks. It can give rise to that deadly mixture of guilt and resentment by one or both spouses. Too often the result is a dangerous and potentially corrosive inequity in the assignment of family responsibilities.

Of course, couples do enter into pragmatic agreements regarding the conduct of their life together. Frequently one person has a better head for finances; another derives more satisfaction from cooking. Often one has very strong convictions about the kind of neighborhood they should live in, while the other feels much stronger about how family leisure time should be spent. What makes these agreements *mutual* is that they proceed from a shared discernment of gifts and obligations. When agreements about marital or familial roles are viewed as if they are etched on stone tablets by God, the mutuality of the relationship can be threatened.

I once worked with a colleague who was having a disagreement with her spouse over their children's education. The husband felt they should attend a Catholic school, while she was convinced the local public school offered a better overall education and that the couple together, both committed Catholics, could provide adequately for the children's Christian formation. He eventually deferred to her because he knew she was both better informed on the matter (she had personally visited both schools, interviewed teachers, and examined curricula) and much more passionately committed to her viewpoint than he was to his. In another situation, the wife might be the one who would defer. The point is that deference to the other emerges out of love and respect for one's spouse and not out of some social expectation or reluctant accommodation.

There are solid reasons for my view that a hierarchically structured marriage depends less on biblical warrants and more on a fundamentalist interpretation of certain key biblical passages. It is true that Saint Paul seems to have accepted certain cultural assumptions about women in, for example, 1 Corinthians 11:3–16, in which he argues that women ought to keep their heads veiled when in prayer. Paul accepts the dominant cultural hierarchy, which asserts male superiority over women. This passage is an admonishment to the Corinthians who may have been flouting certain social conventions in the behavior of female church members. Paul argues in support of these social conventions, but his main point is to use this accepted hierarchical structure as a device for asserting Christ's relationship to the Church. Another text, likely to have been written by a disciple of Paul, is found in the Letter to the Ephesians and is perhaps the strongest biblical text in support of a hierarchical structure in marriage. This passage also likely represents some of the dominant cultural assumptions of the time. Yet on closer examination the text may also be revising at least part of those larger assumptions about the "headship" of the husband in the marriage relationship. Let us consider the crucial text (Ephesians 5:21–32):

> *Be [subordinate] to one another out of reverence for Christ.*
>
> *Wives, be [subordinate] to your husbands as you are to the Lord. For the husband is head of the wife just as Christ is the head of the church, the body of which he is the Savior. Just as the church is [subordinate] to Christ, so also wives ought to be, in everything, to their husbands.*
>
> *Husbands, love your wives, just as Christ loved the church and gave himself up for her, in order to make her holy by cleansing her with the washing of water by the word, so as to present the church to himself in splendor,*

without a spot or wrinkle or anything of the kind—yes, so that she may be holy and without blemish. In the same way, husbands should love their wives as they do their own bodies. He who loves his wife loves himself. For no one hates his own body, but he nourishes and tenderly cares for it, just as Christ does the church, because we are members of his body. "For this reason a man will leave his father and [his] mother and be joined to his wife, and the two shall become one flesh." This is a great mystery, and I am applying it to Christ and the church. Each of you, however, should love his wife as himself, and a wife should respect her husband.

This passage is often misinterpreted because of the statement that just as Christ is head of the Church, so too the husband is to be head of the wife.[3] In fact, while the patriarchal overtones cannot be completely overlooked, this passage is much more subtle than is generally realized and challenges traditional notions of the subordination of the wife. First, the passage begins with a call to *mutual subordination,* one to the other. Only after this call to mutual subordination is male headship asserted. Even then this headship is reinterpreted. The author says "the husband is head of his wife just as Christ is head of the church." The husband's headship over the wife was a virtually universal presupposition in the Mediterranean cultures of the late first century. Yet the author of this text takes an accepted attitude and turns it on its head. The point being made is that, for Christians, the headship of the husband is to be modeled on the headship of Christ, not on secular notions of headship. The consistent biblical testimony regarding Christ's headship is that it was not one of secular lordship, but rather one of self-effacing service (*"the Son of Man came not to be served but to serve"* [Matthew 20:28]). It is in this sense that the husband is to exercise "headship." This suggests that the husband is being encouraged not to be a head over the wife in the larger cultural understanding as that of superiority and domination, but rather in accord with Christ—to exercise headship as humble service. The husband is to be the "first servant of the wife."[4]

The overarching thrust of the text is to ground marriage in a covenant fidelity characterized by a love that is understood as a mutual "giving oneself away" to the other. This sense of marital covenant is also evident in Jesus' own prohibition of divorce (see Matthew 19:3–12). It is a prohibition that essentially rejects the Mosaic law's allowance for a husband divorcing his wife (but not the reverse). Jesus' condemnation of divorce affirms the covenantal character of marriage while at the same time suggesting that the wife is not to be viewed as mere chattel to be dispensed with as the husband wishes.

Intimacy

The life of marital communion is constituted not only by the experience of mutuality as we learn to delight in and affirm the gifts our spouses offer us but also in the experience of intimacy. Sexual intimacy is discussed in a later chapter; here it suffices to speak of the broader experience of intimacy in marriage. We tend to think of *intimacy* as an expression of emotional closeness between two people, yet this is not quite correct. Marital intimacy is nurtured when we strive to go beyond a desire for closeness to a genuine vulnerability before each other. It is what happens when I risk opening up my deepest concerns and fears to another. It occurs when two people risk sharing plans and dreams, rejoicing together when they are realized and mourning when they are dashed. This vulnerability is what gives to human intimacy its power. But as is always the case with power, risks are involved.

To draw close to another is not only to affect the other but to be open to being affected by the other. I have learned much from James and Evelyn Whitehead's insightful treatment of this. They note that authentic intimacy requires that those being intimate have sufficiently developed selves. Few things are more dangerous than a person with an insufficiently developed personal identity entering into an intimate relationship with another. The risk, in such situations, is that the undeveloped self will not only be affected by the other, but will be lost in the other. As the Whiteheads point out:

> Without a clear sense of who I am, I have little to bring to our relationship. There is no "me" to give to the process of mutual confirmation and growth. Instead, I try to become what you want me to be, or what I *think* you want me to be.[5]

This observation suggests that we ought to consider carefully, and with some caution, a popular marital image, that of two halves together comprising a whole. Unity is not absorption. It is not a matter of being absorbed into the other or being completed by the other. Neither is intimacy concerned with submitting to the images, fantasies, and expectations of the other, but when two unique selves freely give themselves over in communion with the other. Intimacy is a powerful reality, and it can "annihilate" an immature self without a sufficiently developed personal identity. It is one thing for me to enter into intimate communion with the other with the full knowledge that I am likely to be changed by that encounter. It is another thing altogether to enter into intimate communion with another and lose my sense of self in the process. Authentic marital communion in intimacy is neither the merger of two selves nor the absorption of one self into the other; it is the abiding together of two persons whose identities are both affirmed and transformed as they offer themselves as gift to the other.

I recall an incident several years ago in which I encountered a woman whom I had known as a friend in college. My memory of her was of a bright and enthusiastic person with a remarkable intellect. I recall her genuine love for college life, not so much for the social interactions it offered as for the opportunities for learning. She was intoxicated by the life of the mind. In the courses we had together, she was never content to do the assigned reading but would do all of the optional reading as well and, invariably, she would offer the most insightful comments in class discussion. Each semester she handled with ease a course load that would have crushed me.

I bumped into her at an airport one day, many years later. As we chatted, catching up on each other's lives, I could not help noticing how much she had changed. I am not speaking of her physical appearance but of the vitality and energy that had once radiated from her as she engaged in her academic pursuits. In the course of our conversation, I learned that about six months after I had last seen her, she met her future husband, fell in love, dropped out of school, and married. Her husband had strong feelings about the importance of his being the "breadwinner" and insisted that she neither continue her studies nor work outside the home. Within months of their wedding she became pregnant. She showed me pictures of her children with obvious pride and love. Still, I could not shake the sense that she was not content in her life.

Certainly one does not need to have a college degree to live a fulfilled life. And a choice to be a homemaker can be equally meaningful. There is a problem, however, when a person with an obvious love for academics and learning abandons all that gives her joy in life out of devotion to another. Is it possible that, lacking a sufficiently developed sense of self, she abandoned that which most fulfilled her to be what someone else, her spouse, wanted her to be?

The other possibility, equally resistant to authentic intimacy, occurs with individuals who possess an overly rigid self-definition. In this situation, one becomes incapable of intimacy because of an unwillingness to undergo the changes that real intimacy demands:

> There is too little flexibility in my sense of who I am, too little openness to learn something new about myself or to change. Personal rigidity leaves little room for self-exploration or self-disclosure. And without self-exploration and self-disclosure I cannot move beyond myself toward you.[6]

The sad truth is that very often those belonging to the second category seek out for mates those in the first category, and vice versa. People unwilling to change are naturally drawn to those only too ready to give up their own identity for another.

The experience of true intimacy is one of the greatest gifts of married life. In this intimacy I experience my wife as the one person who knows my deepest fears and stands ready as a "balm for my wounds."[7] I remember early in my teaching career when the annual ritual of reading students' course evaluations would be met with dread. I might receive twenty positive evaluations only to be devastated by the two negative critiques. My colleagues would often laugh at my consternation. Then I would call my wife and read them to her, sensing with relief that at least she knew of the hidden wounds I carried that led me to give a disproportionate weight to the negative comments. Indeed, it is a comfort to know that this other person, whose own story began long before I appeared in her life, has chosen to weave her story together with my own.

Although intimacy is concerned with our capacity to be close to another, this closeness is not always a positive or pleasant experience. It may also mean sharing the pain of another. One of the most intimate moments in our marriage came when we experienced the loss of our first child *in utero*. We had discovered that we were pregnant in February. In mid-May, the day before we were to leave for a trip to Europe, we went for a checkup and the doctor was disturbed that she could not detect a heartbeat. We went for a sonogram and learned that the baby had died in the womb about a month earlier. Diana would have to return to the hospital later that evening to have the dead infant safely removed from her womb, a procedure normally associated with abortion. I still recall being with Diana in the hospital room after the radiologist had left us alone, staring at the frozen image of our baby still on the screen. Diana went up to the screen and silently traced the cross on the image, and we both began to cry. Intimacy was experienced in broken hearts finding solace in each other.

Marital intimacy is ultimately supernatural in origin even as it comes to us in human form. To be in a committed, intimate relationship is to clear that space in one's heart for another, a space that becomes at the same time an interior temple in which God abides.

Companionship

To marry another is not just to acquire a sexual partner or a lover; it is to discover a companion. There is much to be learned from considering one's spouse as a companion. The word derives from the Latin prefix *com-* or "with" and *panis* or "bread." A companion is one with whom a person shares bread.

Bread is an ancient symbol suggesting both the fruit of human labor and the stuff of human nourishment. It is a powerful biblical image. God offers the biblical bread, manna, to feed Moses and the Israelites wandering in the desert. Yet the gift of manna required the Israelites to rise each morning to gather the manna. When they tried to store the manna to avoid the daily chore of rising and gathering the bread, the manna rotted. God's provision had to be patiently received daily as gift, not hoarded and controlled.

In the desert Jesus was tempted to turn stones into bread but resisted, knowing that bread produced with the snap of fingers for one's own sustenance is no longer gift. Yet the multiplication of bread was one of Jesus' most characteristic wonders, demonstrating the superabundant generosity of God. When Jesus taught us to pray, he told us to ask simply for our "daily bread." And, of course, at the Last Supper Jesus identifies himself with bread, becoming food for the world.

To see my spouse as a companion is to see her as one who shares bread with me. This means that in marriage we are to nourish each other. There is a faint echo of this profound commitment enacted at weddings when the newly married feed each other a piece of the wedding cake. This ceremonial action foreshadows a vital dimension of married life.

Diana once participated in a chaplaincy internship in an institutional home for the elderly. While there she befriended a resident, Fred, who was partially paralyzed and was visited regularly by his wife, Josie. She was no longer able to care for him on her own, but she came daily to visit. A proud man, Fred frequently fussed at the nurses as they attempted to feed him, but when his wife arrived, he docilely accepted her ministrations. Diana was quite moved by the sight of Josie gently cutting Fred's food and feeding him bite by bite. In that simple gesture, she encountered the tender companionship of marriage in its most spare and vital form.

The quality of companionship possible for a couple is likely to change over the years of their marriage. Early in a marriage the emotional rhythms often oscillate dramatically. That is, a couple might experience an extended period in which everything just feels right about their relationship. There are fewer arguments, intimacy and understanding come easily, temptations and distractions are few. However, this period is then followed by another, perhaps more arid or filled with conflict. During these times the relationship can feel empty and lifeless. One of the challenges couples face during these years of marriage is that of accepting these rhythms, celebrating the seasons of closeness while not overreacting to the wintry seasons. The good news is that a distinguishing mark of mature, successful marriages is a gradual diminishment of such dramatic swings in the mood of the relationship. The trust gained from decades of negotiating their common commitment helps to level out, to some extent, the seasonal rhythms of their marriage. What results are gentler peaks and valleys.

In this chapter, I have tried to describe some of the salient characteristics of the life of communion for married couples. This life of communion is encountered in the human experiences of mutuality, intimacy, and companionship. It is here, in the warp and woof of married life, that spouses experience the grace of God. Marriage is not "made holy" merely by injecting moments of formal prayer into one's life or hanging crucifixes over one's marital bed. While prayer is vital for cultivating our conscious awareness of God's presence, the graced character of our marriage is found not primarily on our knees but in the events of communion patiently nurtured in the committed loving relationship between husband and wife.

Questions for Reflection and Discussion

For Single Persons

1. In either your own relationships or those of people you know, have you encountered instances when there were real dangers of absorption or rigid inflexibility in intimate relationships? What are some of the danger signs for either of these tendencies?
2. Why do you think people tend to look for a "soul mate" rather than a "companion" in their search for a life partner? What are the differences in these two images of a life partner?

For Married Couples

1. In your marriage, how have you cultivated the mutuality of marital communion? What are the gifts that your spouse offers you in marriage?
2. Are there obstacles that have made it difficult for you to risk being vulnerable with your spouse?
3. How have you nurtured companionship in your marriage? What is the "bread" that you and your spouse share?

Chapter Four

MARRIAGE AND CONVERSION

Americans are marrying at a much later age than generations past and for different reasons. Still, most Americans do view marriage as part of life's natural progression; the vast majority will marry at some point in their lives. However, when I contemplated the decision to marry years ago, it felt like anything but a natural progression. I was thirty years old, almost two years into a steady, contented relationship with an intelligent, athletic, and attractive young woman. Clearly the time was coming to make some decisions about our future together. I sensed that if I was ever going to marry, this was the time and this was the woman. Somewhat hesitant to make a commitment, I sought out a good friend who had been married for several years. Having exhausted our sports-related "guy talk" over a Wendy's hamburger, I began awkwardly. "Rob, was there any one thing that was significant in helping you decide to marry Nancy?" There was simply no way to make a smooth transition to this kind of a question, and I immediately felt embarrassed for posing it. Yet before I could backtrack, he shot back his answer with a confidence that made me wonder whether he had been waiting for me to broach the subject. "She was my salvation." His response, frankly, made me uncomfortable, and I dismissed it. Now, almost two decades into married life, I find myself reconsidering his answer.

Salvation is about more than "being saved." It is not just a ticket into heaven. Salvation is a matter of God's grace working in us here on earth, transforming us into a new creation. I am not sure that this is what Rob meant, but it is clear to me that my salvation is being worked out within the crucible of my relationship with my wife and children. I experience this saving work in different ways. Like most married people, there are times when I find myself overwhelmed with gratitude for the shared life I have with my wife. At other times, marriage presents itself as an invitation to that difficult yet necessary paschal movement from life to death to new life.

Call to Conversion

In her perceptive meditations on marriage, Nancy Mairs contends that marriage is fundamentally an invitation to conversion:

> This [the marriage commitment] was, and has remained, the paradigmatic conversion, infinitely more powerful and penetrating than anything connected with exclusively religious conviction or practice. I might have found another way to God. I might have found a better way to God. But I did not. My spirit has been schooled in wedlock.[1]

This linkage of marriage and conversion is striking. The biblical word for conversion, *metanoia*, means not just a shift in one's views or opinions but a fundamental change in direction. Marriage, Mairs contends, demands change at the very core of one's being. From the perspective of Christian faith, it is a call to enter into the paschal mystery, that sacred rhythm of life-death-life.

I had a very dear friend, Mary Comeaux, who died of cancer while still in her thirties. I recall a frank conversation we shared about three months before she died. I asked her how her faith helped her to prepare for what we both knew lay ahead. She said something quite remarkable:

There are times, Rick, when I am embarrassed to admit how frequently my faith gives way in the face of doubt. I have had moments when I wasn't sure I believed in Christ's divinity, or his real presence in the Eucharist, or even in the Trinity itself. But through all of these times of doubt, there is one thing I have never questioned, and that is that the paschal mystery, the paradoxical logic that tells us that we find life only in dying, is the one indispensable key to unlocking the universe. In the midst of a thousand doubts I have always clung to the witness of Jesus that there can be no rising without dying.

Mary did not fear her approaching death because she had embraced death, not as the final punctuation mark to her life story but as a raw fact of her daily existence. Mary knew that the life of communion to which we are all called can be fully realized only when we are willing to enter into the paschal movement of dying and rising.

Marriage and the Paschal Mystery

We do not learn much about the paschal mystery and married life in our larger culture. We certainly do not get much of this on daytime soap operas or *Desperate Housewives*. There is plenty of marital dying, to be sure, but it is usually a foreshadowing of some quick marital exit. Paschal "dying" is an altogether different matter. Our cultural obsession with romance and passion has done much to obscure the paschal character of Christian marriage. Yet it is virtually impossible for a marriage to survive the inevitable tests, obstacles, and challenges that will come before it unless the couple grasps the paschal character of their endeavor.

Consider the relatively common experience in marriage of being misunderstood. When I have an argument with my colleagues at work, I can always leave the workplace and the discomfort that the disagreement generated. I can go home, grouse about the dispute a bit with my wife, and then take refuge in my family life, emotionally far removed from my job. If things become bad enough, I can seek a transfer to another department or even look for a new job. In marriage, it is much harder to find refuge from misunderstanding, disagreement, or conflict. I may storm out of the house after a heated argument with my wife, but I have to return eventually. The source of disagreement and the experience of being misunderstood cannot be avoided with the ease that I can avoid the discomfort of the workplace. Moreover, the experience of deep misunderstanding in marriage is quite different from the experience of disagreement or conflict with colleagues in the workplace. For one thing, my expectations for marriage are much higher. After all, I did not accept my job expecting that all of my colleagues would become my "best buddies." I did not take the job expecting that my colleagues would be an emotional salve when I am hurt or an anchor for me in times of doubt. The evaluation of my job performance rarely takes into account whether I have offered my assistant a sympathetic ear.

In marriage, however, these are precisely the things I expect of my partner, and when they are not present in our marriage, the pain and loss is acute. Despite our closeness, my wife and I view our shared world in notably different ways. It is not that our values are different, but rather that we construe events differently and give a distinct priority to the tasks we face. Let me offer a fairly trivial example. My own penchant for order leads me to take on the least pleasant projects first in my life. I have to complete all outstanding tasks before I can allow myself the pleasure of relaxation. For example, when we return from a trip, I must unpack all of my bags before I can flop on the bed and rest. My wife, however, will unpack her bag when she actually *needs* those clothes! She possesses a unique capacity to enjoy the present moment, putting aside all but the most necessary of tasks for another time. At the same time, it also means that she tends to leave a lot of tasks unfinished. Her still-packed suitcase might sit in the middle of our bedroom for several weeks. It would be easy to speak of this kind of difference as an experience of "complementarity" in our marriage relationship but, in point of fact, we usually experience it as an irritating difference, pure and simple. In my lesser moments, I am wholly convinced that Diana's life would be happier and more fulfilling if she would adopt more of my attitude toward life. In fact, I still harbor the illusion that she is my own personal "work in progress" and fantasize of the day when she comes around to the inherent superiority of my point of view! I feel confident that she holds similar views about me.

These differences between us may, in fact, be the very nodal point of my conversion. The place of difference and disagreement is the spiritual place where I am called to a kind of dying, to a vulnerability in which I must try to enter sympathetically into *her* perspective. I am called, without rejecting all that I value, to put aside, if only for a moment, all of my treasured competencies and proven ways of doing things and entertain her viewpoint. This is a risky venture for me because so much of my self-worth is wrapped up in assumptions about the intrinsic superiority of my worldview. This experience of being stretched by the otherness of one's spouse is, I am convinced, an experience of nothing less than God's saving work in us.

The possibility of conversion occurs in these experiences of misunderstanding and the clashes that develop as we discover that we often construe our lives in very different ways. Each of us brings into our marriage private wounds and habits of relating that will need to be challenged. The vocation of marriage is indeed a calling (the root meaning of "vocation") to be stretched, drawn out to an emotional and relational "far country." There is another biblical term for what is demanded here, *kenosis*. Saint Paul used the term to describe what it was for Christ to abandon all divine prerogatives in order to enter fully into the experience of being human. For those who fulfill our baptismal call to follow Jesus in and through the sacrament of matrimony, *kenosis* is the call to a self-emptying or dying to our own needs, hopes, and expectations. It is also a call to attend to this person who, at any given moment, can appear to me as disturbingly other. This is one of the great paradoxes of marriage: a relationship so often sought because of its intimacy, in fact can confront us with our partner's shocking otherness. I am challenged to view my wife not as a cipher to be decoded but as a person to be embraced as mystery.

Marriage as an Ascetical Vocation

Without a doubt, marriage vows entail limitation. Once married, it is more difficult to decide at the last moment to spend a summer in Europe skiing with college buddies. There no longer is an exchange of phone numbers at a party or singles' bar. In our culture, which celebrates the maximization of choice, many young married people chafe against these limits. This in part explains our high divorce rate. How does the Christian tradition help us see this constrained freedom as a positive reality?

In the early Church, those who were executed because of their Christian faith were called *martyrs*, believers whose deaths offered a profound and dramatic testimony to the Christian way of life as a free embrace of the dying and rising of Christ. As widespread Christian persecution died out, the dramatic witness of the early martyrs eventually gave way to the witness of monks and others who set themselves apart from the world for the sake of the gospel. These figures sought to imitate the *kenosis*, or self-emptying, of Christ. They would fast or abstain from sexual relations, not because they believed that food and sex were bad in themselves (though some did seem to hold rather negative views of sex), but because they believed that these renunciations allowed them to better enter into the paschal mystery. This discipline of renunciation was often referred to by ancient spiritual writers as *askesis,* from which we get the word *asceticism*. If Christian asceticism often has been associated with unhealthy exercises in self-mortification, the essential truth was nevertheless preserved that in the Christian life, pain, suffering, emptiness, loneliness, and even boredom—the so-called negative characteristics of human existence—must be embraced as part of the fabric of our lives. Only through the free embrace of these negativities of human existence could life's graciousness likewise be embraced.

Marriage, too, is an ascetical vocation. Frankly, even in our churches, not enough is said about the ascetical character of marriage. When I was growing up attending Catholic schools, the teachers often spoke of three possible Christian vocations: priesthood (though only the boys were presented with this option!), consecrated religious life (life as a "sister" or "brother"), or marriage. The single life, regrettably, was not viewed as a distinct vocation, but merely an interim state prior to committing to one of the three basic options. As the three vocational alternatives were generally presented, marriage was associated with parenthood and spousal intimacy, while the priesthood and consecrated religious life were presented as the more heroic options because of the asceticism they demanded.

Yet faithful Christian marriage has an undeniably ascetical dimension. Those who choose to marry also embrace a vowed life. Marriage draws them as well into a public commitment to enter into the paschal mystery through a real renunciation of goods. Those who would consider marriage renounce the breadth of relationships possible as a single person in favor of the exclusive marital intimacy to be cultivated with their spouse. This is a freely chosen limitation and might be characterized as a choice to explore the *depth* of human experience with this one person over the *breadth* of human experience that can be explored prior to a marital commitment. In marriage, one forsakes the exploration of intimate relationships with a number of different persons in exchange for the unique relationship with his or her spouse.

Although a spouse brings significant personal gifts to a marriage, those gifts are finite and, in time, each spouse becomes aware, often painfully aware, of what the other partner does not and cannot give. For every time that one's spouse is graciously present and attentive in a time of need, there is a time of real or emotional absence. If the sexual intimacy of marriage is a most tender grace, the experience of sharing a marriage bed with one who at this particular moment may not understand me can be terrifying in its loneliness. As Ronald Rolheiser put it, "It is painful to sleep alone but it is perhaps more painful to sleep alone when you are not sleeping alone."[2] There is a paschal "dying" that married couples must embrace in the inevitable experience of loneliness that misunderstanding, disagreement, or conflict brings.

Before marriage, single adults experience a certain freedom to bestow their time, finances, affection, and attentiveness on those they chose when they chose. In marriage, and particularly in marriage with children, spouses are confronted every moment of their lives with claims made upon them by others: claims on time, finances, affection, and simple attentiveness. Claims can and are made on what was once subject to the free disposition of the individual. Bills come in, children need to be diapered at 3:00 AM, a spouse needs to talk about the events of the day. The spirituality of marriage is shaped by one's response to these claims.

An adequate Christian understanding of marriage must emphasize the significance, not only of marital intimacy but also of a sense of absence and the embrace of the limits of the relationship. When these are not embraced, infidelity can result. Of course, infidelity takes many forms. It may be expressed in an adulterous relationship or in the many "small exits" by which one avoids the inevitable experiences of emptiness, disappointment, and longing. These "small exits" can include something as serious as alchoholism and substance abuse or something as innocuous as television, sports, working out at the gym, a bridge club, or children's activities. These activities, many of which can be legitimate in themselves, risk becoming ways to escape the relationship and thereby avoid the emptiness and loneliness that married life occasionally brings.

I have a friend who some years ago shared with me something of the struggles he was experiencing in his marriage. He had graduated from law school as a brilliant and promising lawyer. His professional future was bright. Then he married, and he and his wife had several children. He came to realize that if he was to fulfill his responsibilities to his wife and children, he would not be able to put the time into his career that he had once hoped. He had to let go of the dream of ever becoming a partner in his firm. This was a bitter pill for him to swallow because he knew that he did not lack either the ability or the drive. He began to see a therapist and at one point she asked him a curious question: Did he have a bachelor's party with his friends on the eve of his wedding? He was puzzled by the question but admitted that, no, he had not. He and his wife believed that such parties tended to be sexist and suggested a negative view of marriage as a "ball and chain." Consequently, the couple decided to have a joint party with their best friends.

The therapist gently suggested that this decision might have been a mistake. The importance of such parties, she contended, is that they can help us honestly mourn the passing of a life that we will have no more. This does not mean that we embrace the view that our spouse will be a "ball and chain." It does mean, she contended, ritually acknowledging with friends that a way of life, a life full of unlimited choice and the widest possible range of human experience, will now be renounced. In its place, the soon-to-be-married person will now begin a new life constituted by a lifelong commitment to spouse and children in service of the larger community and the world at large. When spouses freely accept the limits of the marital relationship, when they choose to love even out of the emptiness, they enter into the paschal rhythm of life-death-life and work out their salvation.

"You Always Marry the Wrong Person"

I know a college theology professor who has a reputation for beginning his course on marriage each semester by saying: "It is a fundamental axiom of marriage that we always marry the wrong person." The statement was guaranteed to shock the students, but it contained a profound insight. As we noted in the first chapter, the myth of "the right one" encourages us to look for Mr. or Ms. Right, the person of my destiny. And for a time the intoxication of romance and the highly erotic charge of our initial sexual attraction to our beloved confirms the "rightness" of our betrothed. But over time, as the flush of the initial romance fades in the early years of marriage, the onset of children may dampen the opportunities for spousal intimacy and spontaneity.

Sexual familiarity replaces the erotic charge of the honeymoon, and one's convictions about the "rightness" of one's spouse may be questioned. As basic marital expectations and relational needs go unmet, one or both partners begin to wonder whether or not a "mistake" was made in their choice of their spouse. Quite often a third party arrives on the scene, possessing all the qualities lacking in one's spouse, and now the third party is seen as the "right person" and one's spouse as the "wrong person."

Our professor's axiom suggests that engaged couples would do better to enter into their commitment with a steely-eyed understanding that in some sense they are "marrying the wrong person" and that this reality in no way undermines the legitimacy of this marriage. Indeed, the acceptance of the apparent "wrongness" of one's spouse can provide the opportunity for transformation and growth. (Let me hasten to add that the "wrongness" of one's spouse that I have in mind is not at all to be confused with the wrongness of an abusive spouse—a situation that should never be simply tolerated or endured.)

There is a line of thought in marriage and family therapy that confirms this insight. An expert in marriage therapy, Augustus Napier, in his book, *The Fragile Bond*, suggests that we are motivated in our choice of marriage partner by the highly idealized image of the "good parent" that we constructed long ago in our early childhood.[3] This theory is far removed from the simplistic "males try to marry a woman like their mother" and "females try to marry a man like their father." The theory espouses that all of us face fundamental issues growing up in our family of origin. Not all of these issues are fully resolved in our childhood. For some of us, the issue was about self-esteem and acceptance; for others it was about dealing with authority. The point is that when we marry, at a deep and rarely conscious level, we seek someone who will help us address these issues. We look to our would-be spouse as the "magic partner" who will heal our wounds. Thus, the core issues of our childhood are, as likely as not, to be reenacted in our marriage

...because of the person we have chosen to marry; for we seem powerfully drawn to marry someone who will help us recapitulate those early struggles with our parents. We may think we are marrying someone very different from our parents...but the likelihood is that we will find ourselves forced to deal in our marriage with the core themes and struggles of our early life.[4]

This is not a bad thing, Napier insists, because we enter into this relationship in the hope, not merely of reenacting childhood conflicts, but of healing them. My spouse gives me an opportunity to develop an alternative pattern of response to that which I adopted as a child. Now the irony of this situation is that at some point, when the reenactment of childhood conflicts occurs and our spouse begins to act alarmingly like our primary caregivers of long ago, we immediately assume that we made a mistake. We recall acutely the pain of such conflicts in our past, and we do not want to experience that pain again. When our spouse refuses to change, we are inclined to assume that he or she is not "right" for us. We fail to recognize that this situation is precisely the opportunity that, at an unconscious level, we sought when we chose our spouse in the first place. It is an opportunity to change not our spouses but ourselves, to become persons capable of responding differently to a painful situation. The possibility for change and growth comes only when we acknowledge that the primary source of our growing unhappiness in the marriage lies not with our spouse but with our own unresolved issues.

Let me offer a personal example of this dynamic. I was raised in a family governed by the principles of reward and punishment with very little unconditional affirmation. The typical "firstborn" child, I was raised to be responsible and perform in order to obtain my parents' approval. When I first met Diana, I was attracted to her in part because she did not seem very interested in my academic accomplishments. I was intrigued by the possibility that she saw something deeper within me that she valued. However, since we have been married, I tend to approach her seeming lack of interest in my career accomplishments in the light of my childhood need for my parents' approval. I seek her affirmation of my successes, just as I sought that affirmation from my parents. When she refuses to be drawn into that way of relating to me, I become wounded and can be reduced to adolescent pouting. Our marriage becomes salvific for me when I am able to recognize in these situations a call to go beyond the patterns of relating I brought into our marriage from my family of origin. To put the matter bluntly, my relationship with Diana demands that I grow up!

Marriage as Covenant

Christianity holds that what is unique about Christian marriage is the view that marriage is not merely a social contract between two people but a commitment that is grounded in God's covenantal commitment to Israel and Christ's love of the Church. When Catholics speak of a marriage as a sacrament, they are drawing, in fact, on this covenantal perspective.

In the Hebrew Scriptures there is no developed theology of marriage. However, what we do have is the use of the marriage relationship as a metaphor for God's covenantal relationship with Israel. This is developed in Ezekiel (see chapter 16) and in the Book of Hosea in which the story of faithful Hosea's pursuit of Gomer, despite her harlotry, is meant to symbolize God's fidelity with Israel. It is quite difficult to recover this sense of covenant in a contemporary culture so dominated by a primarily contractual understanding of commitment. In an oft-quoted article on Christian marriage, theologian Paul Palmer contrasts the notion of "contract" with that of "covenant":

> Contracts deal with things, covenants with people. Contracts engage the services of people; covenants engage persons. Contracts are made for a stipulated period of time; covenants are forever. Contracts can be broken, with material loss to the contracting parties; covenants cannot be broken, but if violated, they result in personal loss and

broken hearts. Contracts are secular affairs and belong to the market place; covenants are sacral affairs and belong to the hearth, the temple, or the church. Contracts are best understood by lawyers, civil and ecclesiastical; covenants are appreciated better by poets and theologians. Contracts are witnessed by people with the state as guarantor; covenants are witnessed by God with God as guarantor. Contracts can be made by children who know the value of a penny; covenants can be made only by adults who are mentally, emotionally, and spiritually mature.[5]

Covenant is ultimately about self-gift and involves a commitment to the other that must come from the core of my being. Marriage is such an ancient and widespread social institution that we are inclined to miss how radical this notion of marriage is.

Given the influence of consumerism on our understanding of marriage today, perhaps a consumer analogy is apropos. Imagine that you go to a car dealership to purchase a car. You find the car you are looking for and meet with the business manager to sign the papers. Everything is going smoothly until you come to the final page of the paperwork. It is a document that gives the dealer permission to come to your house at any point over the period that you own the vehicle and replace the car with another vehicle of a randomly chosen year, make, and model. It could be a substantial upgrade (say a 2007 Lexus IS 350) or a substantial downgrade (a 1969 Ford Pinto), and you will have no say in the decision. Who would buy a car under these circumstances?

Yet that choice suggests something of the kind of commitment that we enter into when we covenant to marry another person. It is easy to forget this when I promise myself to my beloved in the wedding ceremony. I may believe that I am promising myself to the woman standing opposite me. Such a promise seems quite reasonable and well grounded. I am sure that I really know this woman. We have talked for hours together on all manner of topics. A commitment to her seems a reasonable decision. Indeed, one of the most common mistakes we make in marriage is our facile assumption that we really "know" this other person, even in the present. The truth of the matter is that in a truly covenantal marriage one promises oneself to a mystery, to a person of infinite depth who is never fully known or "figured out." In his short essay, "On Charon's Wharf," Andre Dubus remarks of his wife, "each day she is several women, and I am several men." Dubus suggests that in matters of the heart, perhaps the complete understanding of our partner is overvalued:

> ...we place knowing and understanding higher than love, and failing at the first two, as we sometime must, we believe we have failed at the third. Perhaps we have not. But when you believe you no longer love, you no longer do.[6]

In covenantal marriage, then, we promise fidelity to the mysterious "other" who stands before us, both wonderfully familiar and frighteningly strange.

Here is where Christian faith and therapeutic insight come together. We hold that when we are faithful to the covenant of marriage and embrace this person to whom we have promised ourselves as the mysterious key to our salvation, God's grace is able to do its work in us.

It is perhaps unavoidable that my description of this process of conversion in marriage appears rather stark and negative. But this would be misleading, for it is also true that when we freely choose to live within the confines of a commitment made to this one person in covenantal love, there is a wonderful sense of liberation. We are liberated from the illusory fantasies of hypothetical relationships and unrealized choices in order that we might embrace the blessings of a real relationship with another flawed human being.

This insight is at the heart of the hilarious yet insightful novel by Nick Hornby, *High Fidelity*.[7] The novel offers a kind of male confessional that recounts the humorous story of a music "geek," Rob, who is in his mid-thirties, single, and owns his own record store. Along with his motley group of coworkers, Rob eats, drinks, and breathes pop music. They spend much of their time coming up with idiosyncratic top five lists (for example, the top five songs about death) and, in fact, use pop songs as a way of making sense of their lives. As Rob tells his story, we are introduced to a narcissistic and self-absorbed young man incapable of acknowledging his own responsibility for the failed relationships of his past. His latest girlfriend, Laura, has just moved out, and he is bitter and defensive about the breakup.

It becomes evident, as the novel progresses, that he "has issues," as they say, regarding commitment. His highly charged fantasy life stands as an obvious obstacle to sustaining a meaningful relationship. Not surprisingly, he fantasizes about having a relationship with a musician. He imagines her trying out new songs on him and making oblique references to him in the liner notes of her latest CD. However, when he is faced with the possibility of actually having an affair with a real musician, he becomes uneasy and is reluctant to proceed for fear that the real sexual encounter could not possibly live up to the thrill of the imagined *possibility* of such an encounter. He admits to the inevitable disillusionment he has experienced whenever he has lived with a woman because his romantic and even erotic fantasies of their life together could not be sustained. When Laura, his former girlfriend, confessed to him that she was not good at being romantic and "slushy," as she put it, Rob observed:

> That, to me, is a problem, as it would be to any male who heard Dusty Springfield singing "The Look of Love" at an impressionable age. That was what I thought it was going to be like when I was married....I thought there was going to be this sexy woman with a sexy voice and lots of sexy eye makeup whose devotion to me shone from every pore. And there is such a thing as the look of love—Dusty didn't lead us up the garden path entirely—it's just that the look of love isn't what I expected it to be. It's not huge eyes almost bursting with longing situated somewhere in the middle of a double bed with the covers turned over invitingly; it's just as likely to be the look of benevolent indulgence that a

mother gives a toddler or a look of amused exasperation, even a look of pained concern. But the Dusty Springfield look of love? Forget it.[8]

This moment of recognition signals the beginning of Rob's maturation as he gets used to the idea that "my little-boy notion of romance, of negligees and candlelit dinners at home and long, smoldering glances, had no basis in reality at all."[9]

The turning point comes when Laura's father dies and Rob is invited to the funeral. Even though they are estranged, he is moved by Laura's obvious pain at the loss of her father. "And at that moment I want to go to her and offer to become a different person, to remove all trace of what is me, as long as she will let me look after her and try to make her feel better." Rob acknowledges and, in a real sense, repents of his narcissistic preoccupations. Later that evening, she embraces him in gratitude, "and when she lets go of me I feel that I don't need to offer to become a different person: it has happened already."[10]

Rob's maturation faces a final test near the end of the novel. He develops a crush on a journalist for a music magazine who was interviewing him. They plan a future meeting, purportedly to continue the interview, but with obvious expectations of more. In anticipation of their next meeting he begins his typical fantasizing about the two of them. The nervousness and excitement, the first kiss, the first sexual encounter, and so on. "When I meet her I know there'll be an initial twinge of disappointment—*this* is what all that internal fuss was about?—and then I'll find something to get excited about again....And between the second and third meeting a whole new set of myths will be born." But this time something different occurs. As he daydreams about their future relationship, he suddenly realizes "that there's nothing left to actually, like *happen*. I've done it all, lived through the whole relationship in my head." Rob sees that real relationships require dying to this ridiculous fantasy world. He realizes that his reluctance to commit to Laura lies in the fact that he'll never again experience with her that flush of excitement present at the beginning of any new relationship. "I've been thinking with my guts since I was fourteen years old, and frankly speaking, between you and me, I have come to the conclusion that my guts have shit for brains."[11]

At the close of the novel, Rob meets with Laura and actually proposes. Laura, wise to his notorious fear of commitment, is skeptical. She questions how he can make a decision like this so suddenly. Rob protests and offers her the fruit of his recent reflections on relationships: "Just because it's a relationship, and it's based on soppy stuff, it doesn't mean you can't make intellectual decisions about it. Sometimes you just have to, otherwise you'll never get anywhere."[12] Rob has discovered that moving from one fantasy to another is no substitute for the sublime virtues of a real relationship with a real person.

Doubtless, *High Fidelity* offers a narrative of the struggle to attain mature, committed relationship from the male perspective. Both Diana and other women friends tell me that while they have recognized Rob's attitudes in their own relationships with men, they do not find the issues he struggles with to be their own. I believe that marriage demands conversion from both husbands and wives; however, I suspect that there may be some gender-related differences in the nature of the concrete demand for conversion that marriage places on us. Nevertheless, all of us, male and female, must come to terms in our own way with the challenges and perils of maintaining a committed relationship with another imperfect, broken person.

Conclusion

It is said so often today that it has become a truism, but it bears repeating in this context: love is work. Rainer Maria Rilke, the famous nineteenth- and early twentieth–century German poet, wrote the following in one of his letters to an aspiring young poet:

People have...oriented all their solutions toward the easy and toward the easiest side of the easy; but it is clear that we must hold to what is difficult; everything alive holds to it, everything in Nature grows and defends itself in its own way and is characteristically and spontaneously itself, seeks at all costs to be so and against all opposition....To love is good, too: love being difficult. For one human being to love another: that is perhaps the most difficult of all our tasks, the ultimate, the last test and proof, the work for which all other work is but preparation. For this reason young people, who are beginners in everything, cannot yet know love: they have to learn it....The demands which the difficult work of love makes upon our development are more than life-size, and as beginners we are not up to them. But if we nevertheless hold out and take this love upon us as burden and apprenticeship, instead of losing ourselves in all the light and frivolous play, behind which people have hidden from the most earnest earnestness of their existence—then a little progress and an alleviation will perhaps be perceptible to those who come long after us; that would be much.[13]

What I am proposing in this chapter is that the graciousness and sacramentality of married life are not limited to expressions of marital intimacy. In this free embrace of emptiness and loneliness, of the needs not met and fantasies not fulfilled, we are called to love not only out of the fullness of marital intimacy, but out of the emptiness of marital loneliness. As spouses we are apprenticed to each other in the life of love, or, as Nancy Mairs put it, our spirits are "schooled in wedlock."

God help us to change. To change ourselves and to change our world. To know the need for it. To deal with the pain of it. To feel the joy of it. To undertake the journey without understanding the destination. The art of gentle revolution. Amen.[14]

Questions for Reflection and Discussion

For Single Persons

1. Rilke wrote to his "young poet" over a century ago. Do you think his reflections on love being beyond the young and requiring lifelong "apprenticeship" is true today?
2. Do you think men and women respond differently to fantasy in their relationships?

For Married Couples

1. How have you experienced your marriage as a crucible in which God has been transforming you more and more into the image of Christ?
2. Have you experienced the dynamic that Augustus Napier describes, that is, that we tend to marry into a situation that allows us to reenact basic issues and conflicts from our family of origin? If so, how have you and your spouse dealt with this?
3. Does your experience confirm or deny modern consumerism's influence on contemporary marriage? In what ways do you see the notion of covenantal marriage as radically countercultural and therefore a "daring" undertaking?

Chapter Five

MARRIAGE AND SEXUALITY

I n the adolescent fantasies of my generation (at least for us tes-
tosterone-charged males), the benefits of marriage began and
ended with the prospects of sex without guilt. Indeed, it is surprising how much theological reflection on marriage still focuses
on marital sex to the exclusion of the larger question of sexuality.
In his younger years, Pope John Paul II once wrote some rather
provocative things about conjugal relations, offering perspectives
that would have made his papal predecessors blush. Unafraid to
discuss the spiritual significance of sexual lovemaking, the younger
Karol Wojtyla even wrote of the value of married couples learning
to achieve simultaneous orgasm![1] This is pretty racy stuff from
a future pope, and knowing something of Christianity's dubious
history in valuing sexual pleasure, I gratefully accept his view as a
welcome corrective. I do worry, however, about a kind of romanti-
cism in the Catholic tradition regarding marital sex.

I recall during my days in graduate school participating in a
seminar on contemporary issues in moral theology. At the time
we were reviewing Catholic Church pronouncements on sexual
ethics. One of the women in the seminar was an ordained Method-
ist minister, and at one point in our discussion she exclaimed in
exasperation, "I don't get it with you Catholics! All of this talk of
marital sex as the 'supreme expression of the marriage covenant'
seems so much nonsense. When I think of those events that sym-
bolically evoke the spiritual meaning of my marriage, I think of my

family at worship together receiving communion. For my husband and me, sex is more about joyful play than about making some grand symbolic gesture."

I am not yet ready to abandon the spiritual and even sacramental significance of conjugal relations—I do think we Catholics are onto something here—but as time goes on, I am inclined to believe that the distinctive blessing of sexual intimacy is more a gentle seal ratifying precious moments encountered outside the bedroom than the symbolic summit of marital love. In any event, the proper starting point for reflection ought not be marital sex itself, but the broader and more universal experience of human sexuality. In service of this reflection we can profit from a fresh rereading of a traditional biblical story.

Genesis and the Call to Vulnerability

The Book of Genesis boldly asserts that we are made in the image of God as male and female. That passage, with its familiar account of the creation of the world in six days, is contained in the first of two creation stories found at the beginning of Genesis. The significance of this assertion is explored in the second creation story. The main features of the story are familiar, but I would like to offer a provocative, new reading of this story suggested by the biblical scholar Phyllis Trible.[2] It begins as God scoops up the earth and breathes into it the breath of life, creating Adam, the first human. I have always assumed that "Adam" was a proper noun for the first human who was, of course, a male. It turns out, however, that Adam is not really a proper noun at all but simply the English transliteration for the Hebrew *ha adam* (only later in the story does it become a proper noun). *Ha adam* is itself a word play on the Hebrew word for the earth, which is *ha adamah*. *Ha adam* means simply "a creature made from the earth." Moreover, there is nothing in the Hebrew to suggest that this creature yet possesses any gender, male or female. The first phase of this creation story begins, then, with a sexually indeterminate, solitary human.

God then creates various creatures, and brings them to Adam, this creature-made-from-the-earth, who names each animal, thereby demonstrating its dominance over the animal. Adam's needs for companionship having gone unmet, God puts the "earth creature" to sleep. The result of this divine surgery is not one new creature but two. First the woman, but also a transformed Adam who, in speaking for the first time, now refers to his new partner as *ishah*, "woman," and himself as *ish*, "man." Thus it is through the gift of sexuality that humanity finds fulfillment. Prior to receiving the gift of sexuality, the first "human" was incapable of authentic fulfillment. Its only relationships were characterized by domination and therefore could not satisfy. Sexuality, experienced as a drivenness toward the other whom we recognize as our equal, becomes the means for our fulfillment. Our sexuality is the most profound signal we have that we are social beings; we are made for one another.

As the story continues, another important fact is revealed. As the first man and woman looked upon each other, they were "naked" and were not ashamed. In the Hebrew Scriptures, "nakedness" was generally a metaphor for both innocence and vulnerability. Frankly, the older one gets, the more sense this makes. Over time gravity exerts its force upon once youthful bodies. We begin to sag in all sorts of ways, and nakedness becomes an ever more apt metaphor for vulnerability.

The nakedness of the first humans suggests that, prior to sin, man and woman were able to be naturally vulnerable, that is, transparent and powerless with each other. Grounded in trust and fidelity, the first humans could be confident that the power of sexuality inherent in being vulnerable before another would not be abused. They could risk disclosing themselves to the other without reserve, without deception. Unfortunately for humankind, the biblical story does not end with this paradisiacal state of confident vulnerability.

The story continues. The first humans are tempted by the serpent to partake of the fruit of the tree of the knowledge of good and evil with the promise that they shall become like God.

And so it begins. The heart of human sin lies in the choice to be like God, not by grace as God intended, but by seeking complete autonomy and exercising absolute power and control over our lives. As the story progresses, we learn that as a consequence of this primal sin, the first humans become aware of their nakedness and quickly hide and clothe themselves. Once we humans make an option for absolute autonomy and control of our lives, the kind of interpersonal vulnerability that "nakedness" suggests becomes too risky. One of the regrettable consequences of original sin is that vulnerability no longer comes naturally. Rather than risk the possibility of pain and rejection that comes with vulnerability, we clothe ourselves with various "masks" and "fronts" that conceal our truest selves out of fear that who we really are will not be accepted by the other. We preen and strut, we blush coyly, and adopt a thousand and one poses with studied intent. This emotional and psychological "clothing" becomes a means of manipulation. Sexual gamesmanship begins.

This broken human condition presents the real challenge of marital sexuality. While magazine covers at the supermarket checkout lines trumpet "Ten Ways to Bring Your Lover to Ecstasy," the truth is that sexual technique is the least problematic aspect of sexuality. The real challenge that sexuality presents to us, a challenge as real for vowed celibates and single people as for married couples, is how to develop appropriately vulnerable relationships with others.[3] By focusing on the root issue of appropriate vulnerability, moral theologian, Karen Lebacqz, proposes a new foundation for sexual ethics:

> Any exercise of sexuality that violates appropriate vulnerability is wrong. This includes violations of the partner's vulnerability and violations of one's own vulnerability. Rape is wrong not only because it violates the vulnerability of the one raped, but also because the rapist guards his own power and refuses to be vulnerable. Similarly, seduction is wrong, for the seducer guards her or his own vulnerability and uses sex as a weapon to gain power over

another. Any sexual encounter that hurts another, so that she or he either guards against vulnerability in the future or is unduly vulnerable in the future, violates the "appropriate vulnerability" which is part of the true meaning and purpose of our God-given sexuality.[4]

This stress on "appropriate vulnerability" brings us back to a central theme of this book, namely, that marriage is an invitation to a privileged form of the life of communion. Appropriate vulnerability can be thought of as a necessary prerequisite for that communion. Unless I risk a certain degree of personal honesty in my relationship with my spouse, there can be no authentic communion and, consequently, no life of grace.

The Erotic Power of Marital Sexuality

The heart of authentic marital sexuality is this call to appropriate vulnerability. Nevertheless, we need to consider in more depth the role of that rich complex of interpersonal activities that falls under the heading of "conjugal relations," including but not being limited to sexual intercourse. This is no sex manual, and we will not address questions of technique and sexual performance. We do need to consider the role that conjugal relations play in a healthy marriage.

The place of sex in a marriage relationship can change dramatically over the life of a marriage. Early on, a marriage may be shot through with the eroticism and romance associated with interpersonal discovery. The highly charged eroticism and passion of sex in a marriage is not without its spiritual significance. The compilers of the Hebrew Scriptures adopted what was originally an erotic love poem, the Song of Songs, because they saw in the experience of human eroticism and passion a profound intimation of God's passionate, driven love for God's people.

How beautiful you are, my love,
how very beautiful!
Your eyes are doves
behind your veil....
Your lips are like a crimson thread,
and your mouth is lovely....
Your two breasts are like two fawns,
twins of a gazelle,
that feed among the lilies
(Song of Solomon 4:1a, 3a, 5).

The implications are provocative. The inclusion of such poetry in the canon of the Bible invites the conclusion that the experience of passion and delight for one's beloved can itself be a participation in the love of God. This is a lot to take in. Most Catholic couples can handle, at least in theory, the sacramental significance of their coupling as a sign of the unity of Christ and his Church. But it takes quite a leap to hold that the sharing of pleasure itself, the pure erotic energy between two people and their carnal delight in each other's bodies, is itself a communion in grace. Luke Timothy Johnson offers this perceptive observation:

> Many of us have experienced sexual passion as both humbling and liberating, a way in which our bodies know quicker and better than our minds, choose better and faster than our reluctant wills, even get us to where God apparently wants us in a way our minds never could.[5]

Regrettably, today the "erotic" is more often associated with the pornographic, or at best a "guilty pleasure," and is understood in a negative way. But this is not the root meaning of *eros*.[6] *Eros* names the way in which we humans experience desire as embodied spirits. It is associated with sensual pleasure and with self-gratification and is closely related to human play. This in itself is an important insight. If we affirm that making love can be a profound and solemn symbol of Christ's love for the Church, we must also acknowledge that making love can be just as important as a medium of play and an occasion for humor. For many couples (and ought to be for all?), sex can be an opportunity, in an atmosphere of covenantal trust, to risk a liberating "silliness" so often repressed in the other, more dignified spheres of our lives.

Eros means being aware that there is a playfulness that ought to be associated with being embodied; it involves a delight for oneself and another. Our experience of the erotic dimension of our existence is one of the most basic ways in which we express self-love, but it is a uniquely relational self-love. That is, in the experience of *eros* we experience self-love in our desire for another. We long for our beloved precisely because their very presence is pleasurable to us.

This experience of *eros* is often met with suspicion precisely because of the pleasure-seeking that is implied. Christians raised on the priority of divine love as *agape* are inclined to think that the only love that deserves the name is that which is utterly self-less. Any act of love that is intermingled with pleasure and delight is thought to be a lower form of love. The roots of such a mistaken view are ancient. Saint Augustine apparently held that before the Fall sexual relations lacked any significant experience of erotic pleasure; it was a biological act like any other. Only with the Fall and sin did erotic pleasure come to be associated with sex. We Christians have been struggling to recover a spiritual sense of sexual pleasure ever since.

It is a shame that the Christian tradition was not more influenced on this topic by another great theologian in our tradition, Saint Thomas Aquinas, for his views on the matter were quite different. Aquinas was convinced that before the Fall sexual relations between the first humans were *more* pleasurable than after the Fall.[7] The argument was simple: Before the Fall it would have been possible to enjoy bodily pleasures in due proportion without becoming obsessed with them. Sexual pleasure, experienced in a relationship where vulnerability comes naturally and without fear of hurt or betrayal, a relationship in which one delights in the other without turning the other into an object for gratification, is bound to be more pleasurable because it will be more *human*.

For Thomas Aquinas the task of the human was not becoming "pure," placing oneself above all earthly pleasures, but becoming chaste, an altogether different matter. *Chastity* meant not a rejection of sexual desire, but a reintegration of sexual desire so that it shared fully in the meaning of human love. The chaste person exercised the "sexual appetite" (a technical scholastic term) in a manner that served or expressed human love. Thus for Aquinas, sexual pleasure was not evil or tainted by sin. As he put it, in words remarkable for their theological import if not for their romantic phrasing: "the abundance of pleasure in a well-ordered sex-act is not inimical to right reason."[8] His point was that sexual pleasure was a good and healthy thing as long as it was realized in actions intended not for pleasure alone but to serve the life of love.

The late moral theologian, Andre Guindon, used the analogy of music.[9] If we believe that all of us are born with a certain raw affinity for music, nevertheless it is true that this raw affinity must be cultivated. A trained music aficionado will have more cultivated tastes and be better able to discriminate between good and bad music. As audacious as it sounds, Thomas's theology would suggest that where sexuality is concerned, our spiritual task is not to overcome our sexual appetite nor to brutally master it, but rather to cultivate it in such a way that we become "sexual virtuosos." This should not be understood according to the model of Hugh Hefner. The goal is to become a person able to recognize the appropriate expression of sexual desire in a fully human context.

What is the difference, then, between, authentic erotic desire and that sin Christians have traditionally spoken of as "lust"? The answer is simple. Lust seeks no more than the gratification of a biological drive. When I am moved by lust, the other person is completely incidental to my satisfaction. In true *eros* the other is desired for self-gratification but without a diminishment of the other. The erotic holds together "other-love" and "self-love" in a powerful, creative tension.

Recently, Pope Benedict XVI, in his encyclical, God Is Love *(Deus Caritas Est),* admits the Christian tendency to oppose *eros* to *agape.* He objects to the way in which contemporary society has often appealed to the erotic dimension of human existence as a way of turning sex into a commodity.[10] For the pope, our central task is not to reject *eros* but to integrate it into agapic love:

> Even if *eros* is at first mainly covetous and ascending, a fascination for the great promise of happiness, in drawing near to the other, it is less and less concerned with itself, increasingly seeks the happiness of the other, is concerned more and more with the beloved, bestows itself and wants to "be there for" the other. The element of *agape* thus enters into this love, for otherwise *eros* is impoverished and even loses its own nature....Fundamentally, "love" is a single reality, but with different dimensions; at different times, one or other dimension may emerge more clearly. Yet when the two dimensions are totally cut off from one another, the result is a caricature or at least an impoverished form of love.[11]

This union of the erotic and agapic ought to be the goal of all marital love.

I remarked earlier that there was a danger in much contemporary literature on Christian marriage to overly romanticize the spiritual significance of marital sex. At the same time, we should not ignore the genuine value of marital lovemaking. The physical and emotional vulnerability that making love evokes renders it a singularly powerful way for a couple to revitalize their marriage covenant as a commitment to be present to and for each other. Reflecting on her own marriage relationship, Cristina Traina writes:

> Sexual affection is part of the "glue" that holds us together, providing refreshment in smooth times and expressing love and reassurance when words fail (or worse, harm). In periods when we have felt precariously close to coming unglued, we have later realized, more intimate physical connection would have helped us to bridge or accept our emotional distance.[12]

It is not that this lovemaking is some privileged source of grace distinct from the many other forms of marital interaction. Married couples abide in God's love, whatever the circumstance, when they attend to each other in selfless devotion, placing the other's concerns before their own. But there is a sense in which a couple's sexual lovemaking ritualizes, as it were, the grace of their daily communion with each other. Just as the sacrament of reconciliation as celebrated in Roman Catholicism, for example, renders visible and effective that divine forgiveness that is always available to those who seek it, so marital lovemaking expresses or enacts in a particularly explicit way the grace of marital intimacy the couple shares in their myriad daily encounters with each other. Mitch Finley puts it well:

> Shared sexual pleasure is central to a marital spirituality. Loving sexual intercourse is not just the icing on the cake for a healthy Catholic marriage. It is the cup God freely offers couples to nourish marital intimacy....Making love is basic to a couple's relationship with one another and with God. Regular, loving sexual intercourse is as fundamental to a marital spirituality as prayer is to the Christian life in general. Because love of God and neighbor cannot be divided, when husband and wife cultivate intimacy with one another, they also nurture their intimacy with God. To put this another way, the bodily way husband and wife nourish their love is also the most spiritual way.[13]

Mary Anne McPherson Oliver has sketched out a "conjugal spirituality" that requires that married couples appropriate the spiritual disciplines necessary for them to thrive. Whereas the primary spiritual disciplines of monastic life were those of fasting, solitary prayer, communal prayer, *lectio divina* (the practice of reading aloud the Scriptures or some other sacred text), and common labor, marriage possesses its own unique spiritual disciplines. The two spiritual disciplines she highlights are talk and sex.[14] By *talk* she means the conjugal discipline of meaningful conversation, which in turn requires the cultivation of the skills of "listening, empathizing, confronting," and diplomacy in the face of conflict. By *sex* she means "that extraordinarily powerful uprising which can tear us out of ourselves, carry us beyond our mind and senses, and at its departure leave our heightened consciousness at peace and naturally open to a changed world."[15] While conjugal relations between husband and wife do not necessarily represent the pinnacle of sacramental marriage, making love is part of the spiritual discipline of married life, a discipline that is by turns earnest and centering, playful and silly.

Much has been written lately on the late Pope John Paul II's theology of the body.[16] The pope, in his many meditations on human sexuality, offered an often eloquent account of conjugal relations as an act of total self-giving that embodied in this one moment, all that the marriage itself stands for. David McCarthy's gentle criticism of contemporary personalist approaches to marital sexuality could apply as well to elements of this theology of the body when he writes, "The chief problem in this personalist account of sex is, not that it goes wrong, but that it says too much to be right. Every sexual act is defined as full and total, so that sex has no room to be ordinary." Earnest advocates of this theology of the body, in their laudable desire to retrieve the spiritual significance of marital sex, elevate it out of its ordinary context as one activity among many in a marriage. They forget that as spiritually uplifting and delightful as sexual intercourse with one's spouse can be, it is more than anything else simply one aspect of one's marital relationship, and often not the most significant one. Again, McCarthy puts it well:

> Through any given sexual act, spouses might express love, desire, generosity, frustration, fatigue, or a manipulative intent, but they will do so in the semantic context of a day, week, a stage of life, and series of specific events, and all set within the broader context of a shared life. Any particular sexual encounter need not say anything earth shattering; it need not point to the fullness or full meaning

of a sexual relationship. We need not be completed by our sexual complement. Most sex within marriage is just ordinary, a minor episode in a larger story. One set of sexual expressions may need to be redeemed by another, and can be. One-night stands and passionate affairs, in contrast, need to be earthshaking and splendid because they are the whole story. They are manic attempts to overcome the fact that there is nothing else. The true superiority of sexual intercourse in marriage is that it does not have to mean very much.[17]

A healthy sense of marital sexuality will neither unduly minimize a married couple's sexual relationship nor put too much emphasis on it. The full spiritual significance of a married couple's sexual relationship can only be played out over the life of a marriage.

…And Then Came the Children

As a couple grows in their marriage, their sexual relationship often undergoes significant changes. These changes come with increased familiarity and as a result of any of a number of other factors, the most dramatic of which is the introduction of children into one's marriage. Indeed, I suspect that no single factor has as decisive an impact on a couple's sexual life as children. With the welcoming of children into the home there is a natural redirection of energy and attention from one's spouse to the children. By the time dinner has been prepared and consumed, dishes washed, children bathed, homework supervised, stories read, and children put to bed, the possibilities for sexual intimacy fade in the face of nightly exhaustion. Spontaneous, playful "trysts" become less likely, and many couples struggle with what it means to have to "book" occasions for marital intimacy. For many there is a fear that the loss of spontaneity is a sign of some deeper problem in the marriage. Spouses become convinced that every other couple is having a lot more sex than they are!

Yet changes in both the frequency and "passion" of marital lovemaking need not be greeted with a sense of foreboding. It is often a sign of maturation in the marriage that lovemaking becomes both less frequent and less feverish. The patterns of lovemaking typical of early marriage can give way to a more occasional, warm, and tender experience that becomes in its own way even more satisfying than the sexual "wrestling matches" of one's youth. At the same time, there may be a temptation to rationalize away the gradual disappearance of sexual intimacy in a marital relationship, avoiding the uncomfortable truth that this disappearance may be a harbinger of deeper problems in the marriage. It is not unusual for couples to make love less frequently over time, and sustained sexual abstinence may be required for medical or other pressing reasons. Yet sexual intimacy remains one of the most profound ways in which couples renew their commitment to each other. Given the frenetic pace of modern family life, unless couples make a conscious commitment to preserve times for sexual intimacy, this is often the likeliest aspect of marital life to be quietly abandoned.

Procreation and Marital Generativity

Many of the reflections on marriage and marital spirituality in this volume are drawn from the theological traditions of Western Christianity. The Eastern Orthodox tradition offers a quite distinctive approach to Christian marriage. It views the married couple as a living icon of the Trinity. Consider that in the triune life of God the love between two (the Father and the Son) is not self-contained but "spills over," as it were, as Spirit. The triune life of God is characterized not only by a mutuality of love between the Trinitarian persons, but also by a fecundity, a superabundance in which God's love overflows outward into the world. The doctrine of the Trinity teaches us that authentic love can never be contained in the private commerce of two lovers. A love between two, sustained in the long term, is always inadequate and faces the dangers of fixation and egocentricity. A Trinitarian love is one that flows outward beyond the two. When the marriage relationship is conceived as an icon of the Trinity, childbearing is seen as an expression of the very fecundity of God. When a married couple brings children into the world, they are sharing in the creative purposes of God.

In this theology of marriage, childbearing expresses the broader, generative dimension of marriage, that aspect of marriage in which we experience our love bearing fruit in the world. Yet the generativity of marriage is also realized in the married couple's call to mission, to expansive community. The Eastern tradition does not view childbearing as an obligation of married life (as it often has been understood in certain Roman Catholic theologies of marriage) but as a "felicitous outcome" of the nuptial union.[18] The marriage relationship reveals the inadequacy of a community of two and thus differentiates itself from the often closed relationship of two romantic lovers.

Catholicism's traditional focus on *procreation* in marriage might be broadened profitably by consideration of the marital *generativity* suggested by this Trinitarian perspective. Several reasons prompt this preference to focus on the larger generative dimension of the marriage relationship. First, and most obviously, not all married couples can have children. The Catholic Church's strong emphasis on the obligation to have children has left many infertile couples feeling as if they were defective, second-class participants in the sacrament of matrimony. Second, a married couple normally outlives their childbearing years. It is important that Christianity offer a spirituality for married couples that engages them across the entire life span of their marriage.

The positive insight of the Catholic tradition is rooted in the fact that bearing children is, in truth, a particularly profound and apt expression of this larger call to marital generativity and mission. Marital generativity can be realized in many ways. For some couples, the commitment to generativity has taken form in a ministry of hospitality in which foster children or the homeless are given a place to stay in an atmosphere of Christian love. Other couples have served in soup kitchens or food pantries. Still others engage in formal ministries within the Church or host faith-sharing and Bible study groups. Whatever the case, these married couples are allowing their love to be fruitful in Christian service and mission.

This emphasis on marital generativity and mission is reflected in the transposition of postures that takes place in the wedding ritual itself. At the exchange of vows the couple faces each other, each entering into covenant with the other. Then, however, the couple is presented to the community, and they move from a posture in which they are facing each other to one in which, side by side, they are facing the Christian community and, beyond it, the world at large.

This discussion of childbearing and its role as an expression of marital generativity leads to a topic that has literally reshaped American Catholicism since Vatican II—the Catholic Church's official prohibition of artificial birth control.

The Challenge of Responsible Parenthood in a Technological Culture

One of the most important statements on marriage in the documents of the Second Vatican Council came in its Pastoral Constitution on the Church in the Modern World *(Gaudium et Spes)*. In that document the council offered a theological vision of marriage that went far beyond the largely contractual notion that had dominated Catholic Church teaching prior to the council. The bishops wrote of marriage as an "intimate partnership of life and love."[19] They affirmed that married love is, in its own way, a participation in divine love. They described conjugal love as expressing two dimensions, the unitive and the procreative, without, however, suggesting that the procreative had priority over the unitive, as had earlier Church pronouncements. The council spoke as well of the need for parents to act responsibly in their decisions to bring children into the world as both "cooperators" with and "interpreters" of God's love. Cooperating with and interpreting God's love, the council held, demands considerable discernment, taking into account both the couple's own welfare and that of their children.[20] Then the council warned vaguely against using illicit forms of birth regulation. They addressed this matter in very general terms because Pope Paul VI had promised to create a special commission to consider the question after the close of the council.

That commission, composed of bishops, theologians, and laypersons, overwhelmingly recommended to Pope Paul VI that Church teaching be revised to permit, in exceptional situations, recourse to artificial forms of birth regulation. A minority report was also issued by some members of the commission; it rejected this recommendation, concerned that a change in Church teaching would undermine the credibility of the Church's teaching office. In 1968, in the midst of a broad expectation of change in the Church's position, Pope Paul VI issued his controversial encyclical On Human Life *(Humanae Vitae)*, in which he reaffirmed the Church's traditional opposition to artificial birth control. He argued that the conjugal act was intrinsically ordered to the transmission of life even when conception could not be realized either because a couple was having sexual relations during an infertile period in the woman's reproductive cycle or because of general infertility. Consequently, any artificial intrusion into the sexual act that would render the act "infecund" would be immoral because it would wrongly separate the unitive from the procreative dimension of the conjugal act. At the same time, the pope did approve certain "natural" methods (often referred to as "natural family planning" [NFP]) that would allow a couple to determine when the woman was ovulating and then to abstain from sexual relations during those periods (changes in a woman's body temperature and the viscosity of vaginal mucus can help a couple detect when the woman is ovulating).[21]

In the thirty-plus years since the encyclical, the pope's teaching has been roundly criticized by many theologians, cautiously avoided by many clerics, and widely ignored by a considerable majority of the laity. What are we to make of this situation?

First, it must be noted that the teaching of Pope Paul VI has not been one of those embarrassing pronouncements furtively swept under the carpet, not to be discussed in respectable company. Pope

John Paul II reasserted this teaching without either hesitation or equivocation, and Pope Benedict XVI has followed suit. John Paul II gave the teaching a new impetus by linking it to his sweeping condemnation of the "culture of death" rampant in modern civilization. The new context in which this teaching has been placed merits serious consideration. We live in an age, the pope often reminded us, in which our technological ingenuity has allowed us to conquer disease and improve the quality of life of millions. At the same time, it has created the myth of human domination and control. We have come to view any and all constraints on our freedom as something to be conquered. Technology has been the weapon we have wielded, to great effect, in our battle to gain complete mastery over our world and over time itself. We have become enamored with the ways in which technological gadgetry can free us from the burdens of our daily engagements and allow us to excise the wasted time in our lives previously spent laboring over the trivial.[22] We live in a culture that champions efficiency and convenience as the highest values.

But in such a technological world, what has become of the grace of waiting, the anticipation of the unknown and unplanned, the openness to surprise? Is there not a danger that our preoccupation with efficiency and convenience has led us to cheapen and even ignore altogether the distinctive blessings that come as we embrace the necessity of certain constraints? Perhaps the matter can be seen in a fresh light if we look to the way we use technology, not so much to prevent conception, as to plan for the birth of a child.

My wife and I have had four pregnancies. One ended in miscarriage, in two other pregnancies the onset of labor was artificially induced, and yet another occurred "naturally," which is to say, according to the natural birthing process and not chemical inducement. The difference in the birth experiences was striking. The miscarriage itself was a painful experience of the fragility of life and a sobering realization that we Catholics, for all of our convictions about the sanctity of life from conception on, have a long way to go in learning to attend pastorally to those who suffer the pain of miscarriage.

The experience of waiting for the "natural" onset of labor was unique. We knew the baby could come at any time over the period of almost a month. With every pain Diana experienced we wondered, "Was this it?" And then came the frenetic activity when the labor actually began—calling family and friends, getting the car packed.

By contrast, the two cases in which the labor was artificially induced were far less tense. We had an appointment at the hospital and so knew several days in advance when the labor would begin. It certainly allowed us to prepare for the event and minimize possible schedule conflicts. Yet what made the pregnancy ending in the natural onset of labor so different from those that ended with an artificial induction was precisely that the former was beyond our control. The baby was going to come according to his schedule, not ours. Waiting for the labor to begin was a lesson in abandonment, giving up control of our lives. That is why I think it so telling that today a far greater number of pregnancies end with labor artificially induced than was the case twenty years ago. Of course, many of these inductions are for medical reasons, but more and more are not. I raise this concern with the honest admission that we too induced labor on one occasion for nonmedical reasons.

This experience has led us to reflect more on what is lost in the experience of an artificially induced labor. When scheduling a birth around vacations and business trips is as easy as the scheduling of dental appointments, is there a danger of diminishing the sanctity of the birth itself? Are we losing one of the precious gifts that a pregnancy offers us—namely, the blessings that come when we become receptive to that which is beyond our control? The hard truth is that we cannot plan for or manipulate God's grace.

There are certainly important differences between decisions about the artificial induction of labor and decisions regarding the use of artificial contraception. My point is that both *can* be influenced by our culture's larger preoccupation with convenience. Seen from this perspective, there is much to commend in the consistent teaching of popes Paul VI, John Paul II, and Benedict XVI on the dangers of artificial birth regulation. They remind us that regular recourse to artificial birth control risks becoming another way in which we seek to master the world around us, including the gift of life. They warn of the real danger that human life itself could soon become a commodity like the laptop computer we can special-order on the Internet, made to our precise needs and specifications.

We should also remember that papal teaching does not condemn all means of birth regulation. NFP honors the need for parents to fulfill their vocation to bring children into the world with due responsibility. NFP has much to commend it. It is a method that allows the couple to work in harmony with the woman's natural reproductive cycle rather than relying on intrusive artificial methods, many of which may do harm to a woman's health. NFP also requires communication and cooperation between the husband and wife, rather than foisting responsibility on one of the parties to take a pill or use a condom. While the NFP method does require periodic abstinence each month, these periods can provide opportunities for the couple to explore other ways of expressing their love for each other. For all of these reasons, it is regrettable that official Catholic teaching on this question has been simply ignored by millions of Catholics.

However, not everyone who disagrees with the papal teaching has simply ignored it. For although there is an indisputable wisdom in recent papal teaching, many thoughtful Catholics have wondered whether an absolute prohibition of artificial birth control can be morally justified. These voices are too many to be simply dismissed as faithless and disobedient malcontents. The concerns they raise are real. They note that while recent popes have written of the God-given structure of the "conjugal act," that conjugal act is always engaged in by persons, and those persons to a large extent invest their actions with meaning by way of their intentions. The physical act that takes place in a rape is the same as the physical act in which a husband and wife ratify their love for each other. It is the different intentions and the different contexts that give decisively different meanings to the two respective sex acts. It is simply insufficient to speak of the nature of the act itself apart from a consideration of the relationship in which the act takes place.

Papal teaching is certainly prophetic in its condemnation of the "contraceptive mentality" dominant in our culture in which convenience becomes the paramount value in decisions about parenthood. At the same time, some ask whether it is possible for a couple to be truly open to new life in the context of their whole marital relationship without each individual sex act having to be "open" to life. Many critics of Catholicism's official teaching argue that there are circumstances in which couples, because of financial constraints or personal limitations, simply cannot fulfill their parental obligations responsibly and have more children. It is not a question of a lack of heroism, but of a heightened sense of moral obligation to care for the children they already have and to nurture their marriage.

Is it not possible, however, to honor obligations to responsible parenthood by using NFP? In many instances these methods do work well, but it is disingenuous to present NFP as the panacea for responsible parenthood in all situations, as Mitch Finley has noted.[23] Despite protests by proponents of NFP, the method does present difficulties. The most significant is that the method depends on periodic abstinence. If one includes the period when a woman is menstruating (a time when many couples prefer to abstain from sexual relations anyway), the period of abstinence demanded of a couple in a typical reproductive cycle can range from eleven to sixteen days. This is a considerable period of time for many couples who, if they have children, are already often struggling to keep sexual intimacy alive in their marriage. Moreover, the time when couples must abstain, when the woman is ovulating, is also the time when a woman's sexual desire is most intense. Factor in the circumstances in which one or the other of the spouses may have a job requiring travel for extended periods of time, and the demands of periodic abstinence can be transformed from "an opportunity to find other ways to express their love" into a major obstacle in the marriage relationship.

Many who are not persuaded that an absolute prohibition of artificial birth control is appropriate believe that underlying this teaching is an unwillingness to acknowledge that marital sexuality has multiple dimensions going beyond the procreative, including playfulness, the release of tension in a relationship, and marital sex as an expression of healing and reconciliation. Most married couples will readily acknowledge that the experience of making love when a couple is explicitly seeking to become pregnant is a unique and singularly wonderful experience of marital lovemaking. But the truth is that for most couples, even those in principle always remaining open to new life in their family, instances of lovemaking when a couple is intentionally *trying* to conceive are relatively rare. What is one to make of all of the other instances when couples make love? Do these occasions have no real significance? Moreover, more than a few married couples would reject the assumption that one cannot offer oneself as gift in sexual relations when engaging in "protected sex." Many women report that it is precisely the fear of pregnancy that prevents them from experiencing sexual relations as an expression of their desire to give themselves to their spouse. This fear of pregnancy is often not a matter of convenience or selfishness, but personal health, psychological well-being, or family financial concerns. Cristina Traina, responding to the contention that only a sex act open to procreation could be an expression of self gift, writes: "On the contrary, I am able to give myself most fully to my husband in two circumstances: on those rare occasions when pregnancy is a hope...or when it is not a worry."[24]

It is important to note that most of the voices in the Church who take issue with the official Catholic teaching recognize that there are important values that this teaching is seeking to preserve. As Julie Hanlon Rubio observes, "while contraception makes possible certain sexual practices and life choices, it is not a radical lifestyle choice in itself."[25] They admit that recourse to artificial contraception *may* lead to the adoption of a selfish, contraceptive mentality, but there is not much empirical evidence to conclude that the use of artificial contraception within a spiritually informed commitment to responsible parenthood necessarily leads a couple in this direction. In fact, Rubio notes, a close examination of the personal testimonies of married couples who use artificial contraception suggests that many of them share the same values as those couples who use NFP: the importance of self-giving, authentic intimacy and communication, increased mutuality, and so on.

So where does all of this leave us? For Roman Catholics, the teaching of *Humanae Vitae* is authoritative and ought not be dismissed or ignored. Catholics must make a good-faith effort to embrace the official teaching of the Church, and they should ensure that if they have difficulties with this teaching, these difficulties do not stem from either an inadequate understanding of the Church's teaching or an unwillingness to live according to the often demanding norms of Christian life. In a culture obsessed with efficiency, convenience, and control, the latter is a very real possibility. At the same time, Catholics deserve to know that although this teaching has been taught authoritatively, it is not a defined dogma. Consequently, there does exist at least the remote possibility of error, and Catholics who make a good-faith effort to align themselves with this teaching but find they simply cannot discover in it God's will can follow their consciences in this matter.[26] In any case, this teaching is a sober reminder that with the power to bring forth life comes a tremendous responsibility to form our marriage relationships in ways that stand as a ringing affirmation of the dignity of human life and the blessings that come with the vocation to parenthood.

Nowhere are the complexities of our humanity displayed more vividly than in the experience of human sexuality. As sexual beings we experience a deep longing for communion with one another. Yet as sexual beings we also discover that this longing can never be fulfilled completely by another human being, no matter how much that person is the object of our love and devotion. Our sexuality leads us to engage in selfless acts of love; when distorted, it can lead us to acts of selfishness and betrayal. Our sexuality can yield both our exaltation and our humiliation. In marriage, our sexuality draws us together and, on occasion, keeps us apart. It renders us capable of play, delight, and the risk of vulnerability. As sexual beings married couples ratify their covenantal love for each other in conjugal union. As sexual beings married couples welcome the possibility that the ratification of that covenantal love might yield new life. In the end, our sexuality holds out for us a tentative but real anticipation of our ultimate destiny with God, where play and delight, risk and self-sacrifice, fecundity and creativity all find their final consummation in eternal communion.

Questions for Reflection and Discussion

For Single Persons

1. Do you see any potential for a sexual ethic for single persons in the theme of *appropriate vulnerability?*

2. What is your reaction to McCarthy's claim that the superiority of sex in marriage lies in the fact that sex need not be everything in marriage as is the case in a "one-night stand"?

3. Do you agree with the concerns expressed in official Church teaching that we are seeing a contraceptive mentality in our society that prizes convenience above all else? Do you believe that a couple can practice artificial birth control and avoid this larger contraceptive mentality?

For Married Couples

1. How have you struggled with maintaining real vulnerability in your own marriage?

2. How comfortable are you with the idea that the erotic dimension of marital sexuality is good and sacred?

3. How have you experienced the power of generativity in your marriage beyond the raising of children? What are some ways in which this generative dimension could be developed further?

Chapter Six

MARRIAGE AND THE DOMESTIC CHURCH

Many reflections on a spirituality of marriage attend to the dynamics of the relationship between spouses. Yet, from a Christian perspective, marriage is concerned with more than the love between two people. In marriage, the couple goes "public" with their love, and in doing so, not only promise themselves to God and to each other but to the larger Christian community as well. As seen in the last chapter, marriage is about Christian mission. It is concerned with the creation of an expansive community characterized by shared discipleship in the service of God's reign. One helpful perspective for considering marriage as the creation of a new form of Christian community is found in the ancient conviction that the family or Christian household was an *ecclesia domestica*, a "domestic church."[1]

Christian Understandings of Family

One hears much today about Christian "family values" and it is universally accepted that Christianity is, at its core, "pro-family." But this language of family values has been manipulated in our contemporary political conversation, evoking ideas and convictions that, in fact, bear little relationship to early Christian understandings of family. It may be worthwhile to consider briefly the ways in which Jesus challenged conventional assumptions regarding the family.

Jesus' Radical Teaching on the Family

One of the most startling aspects of Jesus' teaching, and one of the things that made his teaching so distinctive, was his preaching of the coming reign of God. The first words of Jesus reported to us by the author of the Gospel of Mark aptly summarize the core of Jesus' message and mission: *"The time is fulfilled, and the kingdom of God has come near; repent, and believe in the good news"* (1:15). Jesus takes the message of God's kingdom as he would have received it from his own immersion in the Hebrew Scriptures and through the influence of the ministry of John and reinterprets it in significant ways.

As a present reality, Jesus daringly suggested that the reign of God was breaking into history *now,* in his own life and ministry. Many of his parables suggest Jesus' subversive vision of the kingdom as when he responds to the question "Who is my neighbor?" by telling the parable of a good Samaritan, in which a member of the despised Samaritans from the north is offered as a better neighbor than either a priest or Levite.[2]

Jesus also taught that under God's rule, kinship relations were to be subordinated to the spiritual bonds of discipleship. This is evident in the story in Mark's Gospel in which Jesus is approached by his family. When told of their arrival, Jesus responds:

> *"Who are my mother and my brothers?" And looking around at those who sat around him, he said, "Here are my mother and my brothers! Whoever does the will of God is my brother and sister and mother"* (3:31–35).

The gospel of Jesus Christ stresses the creation of a new family, a new household—the household of believers. Our truest identity is discovered in the recognition that God is our Father and Mother and that we are children of God. Stephen Post has noted that early Christians affirmed the positive value of adopting orphans by pointing out that all Christians are adopted sons and daughters of God.[3] All other relations are subordinated to that of discipleship. This teaching of Jesus need not be understood as the renunciation of the family (though Jesus apparently envisioned that some might do so "for the sake of the kingdom"). However, it does suggest that marriage and family must now be reinterpreted in the light of the call to discipleship. If we are to remain consistent with the teaching of Jesus, our treatment of marriage and family as a domestic church must be grounded, not in the blood relations that define the family, but in the life of discipleship.

The Christian Household as School of Discipleship

One danger of considering the family as a domestic church is that one will imagine the "churchiness" of the Christian household to lie in the way in which it imitates one's local parish. Many are tempted to see the household as a church because we have religious statuary and crucifixes (just as in our parish), we worship together, saying grace before meals and prayers before bed (just as we pray together in our parish). These elements of the home are important to the spiritual flourishing of a Christian household, but these objects and activities are not the foundation of the ecclesial character of the Christian household. The Christian household is a distinctive form of "church" primarily because in the characteristic activities of the household, members have the opportunity to be "schooled" in the way of discipleship.

Consider for a moment the characteristic activities of any household. It is in the household that we eat, sleep, bathe, get dressed, relax, and converse with others. In the context of the home we learn basic social conventions, from table manners to the demands of hospitality toward guests. In the home we learn how to be accountable for our lives; we learn when we are expected for dinner (or to prepare dinner); we learn what chores and other miscellaneous responsibilities are assigned to us, and how the smooth functioning of the household depends on the fulfillment of those chores and responsibilities. More importantly, in the household we learn about the possibilities for committed intimate relationship with others and the privileges and responsibilities that accompany those relationships.

The ecclesial character of the Christian household is grounded in this unique and complex set of relations realized within a common domicile. Because in that complex set of relations realized within the household we are engaged in the most basic of human relationships, the impact of the household on us is all the greater. Even the most active parishioner is only at the parish church a few times a week, for a few hours at a time. But we all live a far greater percentage of our lives within the confines of our household.

It is in this intricate web of patterned relationships that constitutes the life of the household that we can better understand the image of the Christian household as a "school of discipleship." To be a disciple of Jesus is to be shaped and formed in the ways and values of the kingdom with which Jesus was preoccupied. Jesus taught in parables and modeled in his actions the prodigal love of God, the scandalously inclusive and generous justice that typified God's reign. Jesus' teaching on the reign of God was much more than a set of precepts to be memorized; it was nothing less than an alternative form of living, a new mode of existence.

Initiation into this new mode of existence cannot be done in a private manner. The Greek philosopher Aristotle held that if you wish to become virtuous, you should surround yourself with virtuous people. We do not become virtuous by memorizing Bible passages, rules, or Church teachings. We become virtuous by being engaged, at as many levels as possible, with other people who live the life of virtue. Gospel values are not passed on so much by explicit moral catechesis as by the way in which a set of values has shaped basic human interactions. And so it is with the household. We pass on gospel values to our children when those values infuse our most mundane interactions within the family. When our children see how decisions are made, how conflicts are resolved, how work gives way to healthy play; how household tasks are undertaken out of a sense of commitment to the welfare of others; how affection and encouragement dominate all family interactions; how challenges, corrections, and even discipline are engaged in ways that never demean but rather affirm the dignity of all—those children are being schooled in the life of discipleship. The Christian domicile or household is evangelical in passing on the Christian faith primarily by the transformation of its most basic patterns of living. The American bishops acknowledged this in their simple yet profound meditation on the Christian household, "Follow the Way of Love":

> The profound and ordinary moments of daily life—meal-times, workdays, vacations, expressions of love and intimacy, household chores, caring for a sick child or elderly parent, and even conflicts over things like how to celebrate holidays, discipline children or spend money—all are the threads from which you can weave a pattern of holiness.[4]

The Christian household offers most of us our first experience of Christian community and socializes us in ways unlike any other social unit. By presenting the most basic and mundane of household interactions as the locus for the life of grace and the work of our salvation, the church of the home participates in the Church's mission to be a sign and instrument of God's saving love before the world.

I believe that this biblical framework for thinking of marriage and family from the perspective of discipleship has much to offer us. It challenges the traditional view of the Christian household as a self-contained refuge from a hostile world. A Christian theology of marriage and family must never be presented as some inward-looking reality that does little more than ward off the evil "secular" influences of our broader society. To be a member of a Christian family is always at the same time to be engaged in the concerns of the broader society.

Hospitality in the Christian Household

The ancient practice of hospitality offers a particularly apt expression of the fulfillment of the call to discipleship within marriage and family.[5] We live in a world ravaged by the mentality of exclusivity: Women, minorities, gays and lesbians, and, above all, the poor, all experience exclusion in our society. This pattern of exclusivity must be met head-on by the practice of Christian hospitality. Hospitality is too often associated with having friends and family over for a meal or with an attitude of friendliness toward those we do not know. The ancient practice of hospitality has long since been transferred to institutions like hospitals, nursing homes, and welfare agencies. Yet a perusal of our tradition reveals hospitality as a constitutive feature of Christian community.[6] For Saint Benedict, offering hospitality to the stranger was as vital to the life of the monastery as was prayer and common labor. Early Christians took to heart the injunction in the Letter to the Hebrews: *Let mutual love continue. Do not neglect to show hospitality to strangers, for by doing that some have entertained angels without knowing it* (13:1–2).

Hospitality pares the concern for justice down to the basics. Those on the periphery of society, those who live on the margins, suffer not only material impoverishment, but the effacement of the human spirit. It is all too easy for these people to internalize the second-class status that society too often accords to them. Hospitality does not merely provide shelter, food, and other material comforts (state agencies can and do offer these things without offering what Christians mean by "hospitality"); it offers recognition of one's dignity as a person. "When a person who is not valued by a society is received by a socially respected person or group as a human being with dignity and worth, small transformations occur."[7] Filipino theologian, José de Mesa, suggests that "to make room, to give space to the unwelcomed in our lives also implies working and struggling for their becoming welcome in society as a whole."[8]

Although most households are customarily constituted by marriage and the fruit of marriage, that is not always the case. Without entering into the contentious debates over the normative status of these arrangements, we must acknowledge the many single-parent and mixed-family households, as well as those founded on same-sex unions. Household communities for the physically and mentally challenged, such as the L'Arche communities founded by Jean Vanier, also qualify as domestic churches.[9] And married couples are called to be Christian households or domestic churches, whether or not they bring children into the world. Nevertheless, for most households the presence of children and parental obligations to those children are foundational, and I think it is important that we consider the ways in which our obligations toward our children shapes a marital spirituality.

Marriage and Parenthood

Certainly chief among marriage's blessings are the children. Diana and I are the parents of four young boys, and in part because of them our married life has taken on a mood and a texture that we could not have anticipated. In Catholic teaching there are three ministries within the one sacrament of holy orders (deacon, priest-presbyter, and bishop); there are times when I think the Church would have done well to create three degrees of marriage: marriage without children, marriage with children, and "empty nest" marriages in which children have been sent out into the world with the ever-present possibility of their return home! Theoretically, the children are distinct from our marital relationship yet, upon appearing, they are often the most visible sign of what our union has come to be. Many of us married with children could secretly confess a dark and desperate time when it was the faces of our children that made us try harder to heal whatever rift threatened to become an unbridgeable chasm in our marriage.

I struggled over whether a book on marital spirituality should address the question of parenthood. Clearly, not all married couples are parents, and I do not want to suggest that their relationship is in any sense deficient because of this. Yet for those of us who are married and parents, it is impossible to separate completely the two roles. I recognize the distinction between my role as a husband and as a father, but I cannot help seeing profound connections between the two. I parent our children as Diana's husband—it is as simple as that. Both relationships involve lifelong commitments and demand firm spiritual foundations. Together these two interlocking commitments to spouse and child provide the privileged context in which I am being molded by God's grace into something new.

Marital Companionship and Parenting

We discovered earlier the image of the "companion" as being ripe with insight for married life. Marital companionship, "sharing bread together," goes beyond the ways in which husband and wife are called to nourish each other. Marital companionship also includes the common labor a couple undertakes together. This labor becomes for them the "bread" they share with the world. In marriage a new community is established (a domestic church) offering the world the shared fruit of the couple's relationship. This is why for many married couples their experience of marriage is so closely tied to their children.

I belong to the first modern generation that considered it appropriate for the father to be present at the birth of the child. Diana and I were never so profoundly "companions" as when our twins, David and Andrew, were born. One was placed gently on Diana's chest while I held the other gingerly in my arms. A similar scene was enacted with our two other children, Brian and Gregory. These children have become our "shared bread," our common work.

I have often been struck by this sense of parenting as a common labor in the presence of several mature married couples whose children have long since moved out of the home. One such couple, Winnie and Wally, would, over dinner, offer us tales of their own struggles raising four boys. As they shared with us their stories, chuckling and exchanging knowing glances throughout, they offered us, with disarming honesty, both their successes and their misgivings. As I recall those treasured meals, it seems to me now that their children were the "bread" they firmly kneaded and patiently baked in their home as an offering to God and world.

Later, long after their children had grown up and left home, they experienced their adult children in a new way when they returned to visit. Stories of these visits, told with the same love and affection, nevertheless were cast differently. The children were no longer living projects to be shaped by parental hands; they were now adults who had gone out into the world where, by turns, they stumbled and flourished. In any case, they returned home as individual adults with their own tales to be told, tales in which the continued influence of their parents appeared less pronounced. These adult children now represented "return gifts" to be welcomed and embraced by their parents. So it is that the bread we offer the world returns to us transformed for our delight and nourishment.

For most couples this marital dynamism of offering and return is experienced in the process of parenting. Yet another couple comes to mind, Sam and Nancy, who were not able to have children but worked for years to start a soup kitchen in their small town. Finally they were able to establish one, and within two years had forged relationships with many of the area churches. This common endeavor had become their shared bread. I know other couples whose children have grown and yet who share common labor in the way they welcome teenage unwed mothers into their home, where they can finish school while they have their baby. Here again we witness bread offered to the world, only to return in new and unexpected ways. Whenever a couple engages in common labor, in service of the church or the larger human community, they are true companions.

This profound movement in marriage in which common labor is offered and returns as gift is enacted liturgically in the Roman Catholic celebration of the Eucharist. In the liturgy the gifts of bread and wine are set on a table in the back of the church and, at the appropriate moment, are brought forward by members of the assembly to be placed on the altar. The priest prays over these gifts a prayer that has its roots in the ancient Jewish liturgical tradition:

Blessed are you, Lord, God of all creation. For through your goodness we have this bread to offer, which earth has given and human hands have made. It will become for us the bread of life....Blessed are you, Lord, God of all creation. For through your goodness we have this wine to offer, fruit of the vine and work of human hands. It will become our spiritual drink.[10]

The bread of the Eucharist is not mere wheat; it is wheat transformed by human hands into bread. The wine is more than grapes; it is grapes transformed by human hands. These offerings are the fruit of human labor offered to God only to be returned as wondrous gift, "our spiritual food and drink."

This brief meditation on marital companionship suggests a way in which the married couple, as a domestic church, a church of the home, is also a eucharistic community. When I was growing up in the late 1960s and 1970s, it was common for Catholic families to invite the parish priest into one's home to conduct a "home Mass" for a small gathering of family and close friends. This celebration of the Eucharist was seen as a wonderful way to "sacralize" home life. When married couples live the life of communion as true companions, the fruit of their shared labor is already a form of "Eucharist" in which "bread" is shared. Parenthood exhibits a eucharistic character.

The "Good" Parent

I have no illusions regarding my abilities as a parent. As a father I seem to commit parenting blunders at an alarming rate. Diana clearly has more of an instinct for this than I do. This is not to say that I am a bad parent; I am simply not an exemplary one. But then my personal standard for being a "good parent" has lowered substantially over the years. In the early years of my marriage, when children were still part of an uncertain future, "ideal parents" were ones who never raised their voices because they did not need to; they spoke with a quiet wisdom that virtually commanded respect. "Ideal parents" never laid a hand on their children, never employed hurtful sarcasm. "Ideal parents" always gave their children their undivided attention. "Ideal parents" patiently explained their actions, particularly as they affected their children.

Needless to say, my standards have changed, becoming considerably more modest. I have abandoned all hope of ever being the "ideal parent." I now aspire to be merely a "reasonably good parent," the chances of success being much improved. "Reasonably good parents" love their children even if they do not always show it. Good parents do communicate their love to their children in both words and gestures—even if these affectionate words and gestures are interspersed with other words and gestures that communicate anger and frustration. "Good parents" are present—perhaps not always emotionally attentive—but present. The child must know that though parents may become angry, may even take on the appearance of an apoplectic seizure, they will not leave them, not today, not ever. "Good parents" acknowledge the importance of the parental "rules of engagement," even if they do not always live up to them. These rules prohibit parenting by fear or taking advantage of the inherent inequity of power in the parent-child relationship. They prohibit a parent from taking out adult frustrations on the child. "Good parents" are likely to break these rules often, but they will display the courage to admit it to their children. "Good parents" see to it that their children know that in their parents they have an emotional safety net under the terrifying high-wire act of childhood and adolescence. Good parents strive to be coach, cheerleader, and team doctor all rolled into one.

I believe I pass this lower standard. Do I yell more than I would like? Yes. Do I discipline out of anger? Yes. Am I ashamed to say that I have acted in ways that at times have led my children to fear me? Yes. Do I ignore their needs and dismiss them when I should listen? Again, yes. So I am by no means an "ideal parent," but I am a "good" one, if only because I long to be one and am determined not to abandon this longing. It also means that I am humbled by my vocation and reminded daily by the faces of my children that there is much in me that has yet to yield to God's transforming grace. Those faces also remind me that my children are paying for this stubbornness.

Revisioning Parenthood

My years as a parent have led me to a certain "revisionist" thinking about the traditional understanding of the parental role. If an authentic spirituality of marriage is to incorporate the wisdom gleaned from parenting, conventional accounts of parenting may require some reworking. I have in mind here three actions I have always viewed as foundational to parenting: providing, protecting, and forgiving.

The Parent as Provider

As parents we have inherited deep-rooted expectations about being a provider to our children. This is not all bad. Many of us learned much from fathers and mothers who taught us the values of industry, responsibility, perseverance, and self-discipline necessary to support a family. At the same time, the stereotype of the parental provider carries with it some dangers. The indispensable responsibility to provide for a family, if we are not careful, can blind us to our need, not only to provide for our children, but to engage them in relationship. I speak freely of my children as "living sacraments," effective signs of God's love. But the hard truth is that they cannot be "sacrament" to me unless I am present to them. We live in a culture that sets up the expectation that we provide for our children at least as well, if not better, than our parents provided for us. In an ever more materialistic culture, provision for our children cannot help but be translated into material provision. It has become a reflex gesture within our culture to express our care in material terms. The best neighborhoods, the best schools, the best clothes, the best sports programs—all these things, we come to believe, are the concrete measure of our success as providers. It is a myth that often serves to justify long days at the office and the inexorable climb up the corporate ladder.

In truth, there is nothing wrong with the view of the parent as provider. The problem is that we tend to become preoccupied with the wrong "provisions." Beyond the bare minimums of a home that protects our loved ones from the elements (meteorological and criminal), nutritious food on the table, serviceable clothes, and safe educational opportunities, our children's material needs are surprisingly few. The most compelling provision required by our children is parental presence and engagement, and, lamentably, this presence and engagement cannot be strictly scheduled.

Herein lies the difficulty with the notion of "quality time" with our children. For me, an example of "quality time" would be the time I set aside to go to a major league baseball game with my boys or to read with them at night before bed. This "quality time" is important. But there is a depth and a texture to my experience of my children that often does not emerge in such carefully planned events but rather in the "down time" when nothing important seems to be happening. An example would be the time, driving my youngest child home from preschool, when I listened to him making up a hymn with a spontaneous and hilarious mélange of disconnected religious images. It was a musical creation I would not have heard if I were using the cell phone to take care of business. Or the time when we were all in the kitchen making pizza and my two youngest boys, Brian and Gregory, each put pots on their heads and ran headlong into each other like two feuding billy goats crashing into each other, then falling down on the floor laughing hysterically.

I am spectacularly unsuccessful in planning "quality" interaction with my children. Invariably, I will ask them some serious question about their hopes and dreams only to be met with a puzzled or even bored look on their faces. No, these interactions generally happen according to an inscrutable calendar in which I have no choice but to wait, being, first and crucially, available and attentive to that random moment when my child suddenly blurts out his greatest fear or proudly shares his greatest achievement.

The grace that comes to us in the lives of our children comes to us as surprise, often in the delightfully unexpected moments: while working on the lawn, preparing a family meal together, or running family errands. The notion of quality time with our children, a notion with origins in time management principles appropriate to the workplace, ignores the fact that quality interaction with our children cannot be programmed. Much of what I have come to know about the life of communion I first learned through my children. To live in communion is to be attentive, in the present moment, to the presence of the other. The life of communion, like quality time, cannot be "booked." The central provision I am called to offer my wife and children is, quite simply, me—fully present and open to discovering the marvelous gift that they are for me.

There is a second dimension to the role of parent as provider that deserves consideration. It concerns how we view our careers and how we present them to our children. Too many of us view our paid labor as a means to a paycheck that allows us to provide for our children. However, if we are to view the Christian household as a domestic church, a school of discipleship, then ought not our labor, paid and unpaid, be a part of our call to discipleship and mission? In the Roman Catholic tradition, we have a developed social teaching on the dignity of human labor as one of the ways in which we become "co-creators" with God, sharing in God's work to bring about the coming of God's reign.[11] If our household is to be a school of discipleship, then part of that schooling is teaching our children that their life's labor ought to be about more than a paycheck and family provision; it ought to be labor undertaken in service of God's reign. According to Julie Hanlon Rubio, the dignity of human labor demands that we consider the dual vocation of parents both to their children and to the service of God's reign through their labor, paid and unpaid.

> Christian parents trying to live as disciples of Christ ought to see work as more than a means to an end, more than a way to support the family. It makes little sense to spend ten to fourteen hours a day getting ready for, getting to, doing, and getting home from something less than meaningful in order to make the other, more meaningful two to six hours of the day possible.[12]

This in turn means that we must reconsider much traditional thought about dual-paycheck households. Many women who wish to be married and have children while continuing to work outside the home are made to believe that they are failing in their obligation to "put their families first." That may be the case when two incomes are sought in order to achieve and/or maintain a more affluent lifestyle. But it is possible that both spouses are working out of a commitment to fulfill their vocation to share in God's work in the world.

> Work is a part of a Christian's commitment to live an ethical life. Parents cannot put it aside when children arrive, nor can they allow the needs of children to shift the focus of work from humanity to "providing the best."[13]

In the modern household, a whole new set of negotiations must be undertaken in which both husband and wife recognize the spiritual significance of their labor, paid and unpaid, and balance this with the need to be present and active in the lives of their children.

The Parent as Protector

Protecting my children is almost as fundamental to my conception of parenting as that of providing for them. Again, seeing oneself as a protector of children is not necessarily a bad thing. It is a great gift to our children for both father and mother to offer them a sense of protection and stability, to reassure them that their home is indeed, both physically and emotionally, a "safe" place. But to a greater extent than I think most of us realize, our role as protector is illusory. This was brought home to me painfully several years ago.

We were returning from a family vacation when we were involved in a serious car accident on the interstate. There was a pileup a half mile ahead, and in the process of braking I lost control of our van, smashed sidewise into a truck pulling a boat, and caromed through the grass median and directly into oncoming traffic.

When I finally regained control of the van and pulled off onto the shoulder, I turned around to see all four of our children crying, and one of them, Brian, bleeding profusely from his head and face. The ambulance quickly arrived and, because the paramedics feared he might have a serious head or spinal injury, Brian was strapped to a gurney and whisked off to the nearest emergency room. It turned out that his injuries were not serious, and he, along with the rest of the children and Diana, was fine. But forever etched in my memory will be the sight of my four children screaming in fear and pain. As the driver of the van, I felt responsible for what happened. At a very deep level, I believed I had failed them. I had broken some unspoken covenant—a silent agreement ratified by countless acts of care—in which I promised that I would protect them from harm. The experience has forced me to reassess my parental identity as protector. It made me realize that, in fact, I cannot really protect my children at all. I cannot promise them that they will never be hurt or feel pain, loss, or tragedy. There is no parental "force field" that I can project around them to keep them secure.

This recognition has not come easily to a person like myself, because, while the desire to protect is good and noble, it often veils a deeper and more questionable desire to control the lives of others. This operates on two levels. On the first level is the pain I feel at the pain of my loved ones. I grew up as a child feeling very insecure as I was often the butt of jokes because of my nerd-like demeanor. In consequence, I find it excruciatingly painful to watch one of my children be teased in any fashion. A forty-eight-year-old man with four college degrees, I can be reduced to the most juvenile of attitudes, wishing to "tell off" the perpetrators of my child's emotional injury as if the battles my children face were the laboratory in which I might finally resolve my own issues. Yet the letting go that is demanded here, allowing my children to deal with taunts and insults, is as difficult for me as it is necessary for them.

As a firstborn child, I was affirmed at an early age as the family "fixer," the one who could intervene in troubled family situations and resolve the dispute. I have carried this "fixer" role into my marriage and family and am still struggling to admit that in many instances what I was trying to fix was my own discomfort and impotence in the face of the pain of someone I loved. Committed love leaves us open to that peculiar pain felt when we dare to "share the pain" of another without trying to make it go away. All I can promise my wife and my children is my attentiveness, my compassionate presence, my commitment never to abandon them in their pain. Indeed, this is all God promises any of us, and to embrace this promise as parent and spouse is to accept our own humble role as instruments of God's compassionate presence.

Abandoning the role of protector is an invitation to enter once more into the rhythm of the paschal mystery, dying to the presumption that I have—or ought to have—absolute control over the ultimate destiny of my wife and children. If I am honest with myself, there is a hubris in overestimating my impact on my children's still young lives—for they, too, are sturdily, resiliently other, a mystery unfolding that I may feel compelled to nudge along but can never wholly direct. I am invited to embrace their own developing life stories as their stories, stories that must be written through their choices as much as by my counsel, protection, and care.

Dispensing Mercy, Offering Forgiveness: Participating in the Household of God

The "good parent" forgives. I know few parents who would not think of themselves as forgiving. I am confident that there is nothing my children could do that I would be unwilling or unable to forgive. Yet recent reflections on a well-known biblical story have led me to consider anew the true demands of parental forgiveness.

We all know the basic plot: a father has two sons, and the younger approaches the father and asks for his inheritance. This was a highly unusual and harsh request in ancient times for two reasons. First, to ask a father to divide his inheritance was essentially to rob him of a livelihood in his final years. Second, because such a gesture represented a dismissal of the father's value to the son, the younger son was essentially saying he could not wait for his father to die. In any event, the son then proceeds to "squander his inheritance." Soon he is hiring himself out to care for swine. So hungry is he that even the pig slop looks appealing. It is at this point that the biblical text introduces a detail that somehow I never really caught before. The son "comes to his senses" and realizes how much better off were the servants at his father's house. An idea comes to him: "*I will get up and go to my father, and I will say to him, 'Father, I have sinned against heaven and before you...'*" (Luke 15:18).

Maybe it is because I now read the text as a father in a way that I never did before, but I am troubled by a question that will not go away: Is the son truly contrite or is he just hungry? Is the son merely plotting: "What words must I offer to regain my father's favor?" My suspicious, fatherly heart wonders whether he is seeking to regain admission into the household but without genuine repentance. I've seen this on the faces of my own children: "What do I need to say to him that will keep me from being grounded?" The point is not minor because, while I can imagine nothing my children might do for which I would not extend forgiveness, I would expect a genuine expression of contrition as a prerequisite for that forgiveness. Yet such does not appear to be the case for the father in the parable. When he sees the son coming at a distance, he does not wait for a profession of contrition but rather, in an action most unseemly for a father of that time, runs to embrace him. It is only after this embrace that the son offers what is apparently an authentic confession of sin.

This parable goes far beyond the world of parental forgiveness that I know. Is Jesus really suggesting that in his Father's house this is how forgiveness works? Are we supposed to extend forgiveness even prior to an expression of authentic repentance? This text shines an uncomfortably harsh light on my own exercise of parental forgiveness where my acceptance and approval become bargaining chips offered in exchange for desirable behavior. The gospel is calling me to something far more radical.

It goes without saying that children must be taught responsibility and accountability for their actions, but this cannot come by the withholding of forgiveness or the suggestion that forgiveness requires prior contrition and penance. I am called to examine whether I am willing to let our household share in the paradoxical wisdom of God's household, where it is not a son's inheritance that is wasted prodigally, but the love of the Father. This wastefulness of the love of God is a central theme in the New Testament. There it is in the parable of the laborers of the vineyard, in which the owner of the vineyard chooses to pay those who only worked a few hours a full day's wage (see Matthew 20:1–16). How dare he? Why waste a full wage when in justice he could pay much less? And then there is the corrupt chief tax collector, Zacchaeus, climbing a tree to see Jesus but motivated by nothing other than curiosity (Luke 19:1–10). Does Jesus confront him with his obvious sins and demand conversion? No, he invites himself into Zacchaeus's house and lets this radical acceptance do its work. It is the very prodigality of this unconditional acceptance, the sheer wastefulness of the gesture that effects Zacchaeus's conversion. This is how it is in the household of God.

When I say that this practice of forgiveness cannot make contrition and repentance a precondition, this should not be understood as condoning a kind of cheap grace in which nothing is expected of the one being forgiven. To extend forgiveness is to initiate the painful work of restoring relationship. This requires something of both parties. As the one forgiving, I am called to initiate this restoration, but the actual restoration of communion depends on how that offer is received; without an acknowledgment of wrongs committed and a commitment to address and change the circumstances that effected the rupture of communion, no real restoration of communion is possible. In the parable of the prodigal son, we do not really know how things end. Does the son truly receive the forgiveness of the father and do whatever is necessary on his part to restore communion (for example, giving himself over to the common labor of the farm, cultivating a sense of gratitude for the father's gracious love)? We do not know. Forgiveness offered is not forgiveness made effective.

Notions of Christian forgiveness have been shaped by our understanding of divine forgiveness. For centuries Christians have spoken of God's forgiveness embodied in the crucifixion of Christ. There is a deep wisdom here, but it has often been distorted because the saving work of the cross was presented variously as paying a ransom (to whom?), forgiving a debt, or absolving guilt. I believe the crucifixion of Christ as an embodiment of God's forgiveness is best understood as an act of reconciliation, the restoration of communion.[14] Saint Paul wrote that in Christ *God was reconciling the world to himself* (2 Corinthians 5:19). To forgive is more than paying a ransom or vicariously assuming the punishment of another, it is more than forgiving a debt; it is an attempt to restore or heal a relationship.

This is what is demanded of me as a parent and spouse within a household committed to being a school of discipleship: to embody God's forgiveness by engaging consistently in the kinds of actions that seek to restore and maintain communion with my wife and children. To offer forgiveness in my household is not to engage in a series of magnanimous actions; it is a way of *being* toward the significant others in my life. This way of being demands that, in the face of actions that risk breaking our communion with one another, I refuse to accept that brokenness and do whatever I can to restore relationships. It is precisely in my imperfect and halting embodiment of God's forgiveness in all of my actions and attitudes that I am made holy, sanctified, saved.

Embracing Our Children as Gift

The Trinitarian and paschal logic of gift must be cultivated in Christian households. Our children present us with marvelous opportunities to embrace our lives as gift. My oldest two boys, David and Andrew, are teenagers now, and I have already begun to recognize some subtle changes. We are an affectionate family, but I have noticed that the older boys are no longer as at ease as they once were with my displaying affection with them in front of their peers. I remember visiting them at their school a number of years ago during their lunch period, and although I knew they were happy to have me sit at the lunchroom table with them, they were less so when I gave them a parting hug. I knew well that what was happening was simply a normal developmental process, yet I felt a sadness that I could not dispel. Two weeks later, the three of us were going to an Astros baseball game when both of them spontaneously grasped my hands on each side as we walked through the parking lot. I acted nonchalantly, holding their hands firmly, while uttering a silent prayer of gratitude, asking only that I be able to treasure the grace of the moment. Our children's faces are canvases upon which a wondrous world of emotions and discoveries is painted as if solely for our enjoyment. They laugh and something long dormant stirs within us; they cry and our hearts break. They grow and we discover, as we nurture that growth, the most sublime of vocations. We are blessed in acknowledging their dependence on us, and blessed again when they grow out of that dependence from children to adolescents and, thanks in no small part to our parental ministrations, become mature, capable, caring adults.

A less obvious gift offered by our children is the way in which they stretch us in such unexpected ways. I derive a tremendous delight from our children, to be sure. Yet I am easily overwhelmed by the emotional demands that parenting makes on me. I tell myself that I would be a great father if I could just submit all of this parenting "stuff" to some kind of reasonable schedule! I keep trying to "manage" this relationship with my kids the way I do with my students. Why can't I establish parenting "office hours"? Yet it is not just the chaos of a noisy household and the emotional demands placed on me by four growing boys that call me to the "dying"; it is the children themselves. Whatever Jesus meant when he suggested we must imitate the children, it had nothing to do with angelic innocence! There is no point in hiding it. Our children, who can so often be for us veritable "sacraments" of God's grace, are also imperfect creatures, capable of the same pettiness, resentment, and mean-spiritedness that sets us adults to warring.

I have come to embrace my children as gift in a special way as I discover that it is they who are shaping me every bit as much as I them. Exuberant in play, fierce in anger, yet paradoxically, quick to forgive, I see in my children an emotional clarity that has long since become jumbled and even duplicitous in me. My son Brian has a temper that I keep trying to attribute to his mother's side of the family! When I deny him a request, I am often startled by the emotional force of his anger. Yet ten minutes later he will be sitting by my side recalling for me some play he made on the baseball field or a school project undertaken with his favorite teacher. From a distance I gaze upon my children and long to know the "cleanness" and purity of their emotions. I lack the confidence in my own emotional life to dare to give it such open and honest expression. And yet there are moments when I shed my status as an emotional bystander and manage to shuffle out of the stands and onto the field of play, wrestling with the boys on the ground, or singing a song with them in the car, that I think, in my communion with them, I may indeed be recapturing some great lost thing.

I wonder if there are people who have brought children into the world who truly have felt that they figured it out, that they mastered the art of parenting. For my part, I feel as if I were on a dinghy cut loose from its moorings and floating wildly down the river. I can make slight course corrections, but it is the river that is in charge. I offer those I love most, my wife and children, good intentions, flawed actions, and the commitment to stay the course, even as I hear raging rapids just around the bend. My married life has much the same feel. I am career professional, spouse and parent, husband and father—inseparable vocations. All of them call forth from me more than I possess. All bless me with more than I deserve.

Questions for Reflection and Discussion

For Single Persons
1. As you consider your own family situation, in what ways did your family resemble a domestic church?
2. How do you see your own chosen profession as a work in service of God's reign?

For Married Couples

1. What are some concrete ways in which your role and responsibilities as a parent have affected your marriage relationship?
2. How has this chapter challenged you to rethink your role as provider, protector, and forgiver?
3. As specifically as you can, try to list all the ways in which you have experienced your spouse and children as gift.

Epilogue

Some time ago our family was in the midst of making a major transition, moving from Houston to Toledo, Ohio. We were leaving not just the state of Texas, the state in which Diana was born and raised, but the state that had, in adulthood, become my adopted home. Almost all of our extended family lived there, as did most of our closest friends. The transition itself was a curious mixture of excitement, sadness, and stress. There was a house to be sold and another to be purchased, furniture to move, ten years of accumulated stuff to sort through and pack, a series of "one-last-time" breakfasts and lunches with friends to be had.

When you live in one place for an extended period, marriage and family life take shape within a larger, more comprehensive network of relationships. They blend together, intertwine, often in ways unnoticed until a move is contemplated. Telephones, e-mail, the postal service, and cheap airfares guarantee that such transitions need not be as final a break as they were for generations past. Still, when everyone piles into the van and waves goodbye, it hits you in the gut that, within the larger circle of family and friends, some are going and some are not. A family move becomes a stark reminder that however much I have drawn sustenance and support from my extended family and friends, in the end, vows made long ago mean I have cast my lot with this noisy crew. We were bound together, and this bond was both a source of great comfort and a bit unsettling. Any one of us, parent or child, might, if we had thought about it, have looked around and wondered about what might have been, had different choices cast us with a different group of people. But it is idle speculation and we know it. These are our people for good or ill. This book has been an extended meditation on the spiritual significance of belonging to such a community.

I would like to conclude this volume with brief reflections on two topics that, perhaps surprisingly, have not received much attention in these pages: prayer and fidelity. Thomas Merton once wrote: "A tree gives glory to God by being a tree."[1] It is simply by being what they are that trees glorify God. With us it is different. We humans give glory to God by becoming the children God has called us to be. We glorify God in the exercise of our freedom shaped by lives of prayer. It may seem odd that in a book described as an exploration of spirituality there has been so little said about conscious prayer. This should not be interpreted as low regard for the importance of formal prayer. I have found, paradoxically, that as our marriage has proceeded, the hunger for personal prayer has grown. The frenetic pace of our home life has fueled a desperate need to begin each day with a time of solitude in which I set down roots in the love of God. The question of technique continues, and I claim no expertise on this score, but I am convinced that matters of prayer technique are overrated. I have a very dear friend of almost two decades who, ever since I have known him, has spent his time in morning prayer silently reading the Gospel of Mark over and over as he paced about the house—without commentary, without journals, without the tools of imaginary prayer often recommended in prayer workshops. He himself would admit that he might easily have chosen another method. What was vital was the sense of a daily grounding in God's presence.

Diana and I continue to struggle with the goal of praying together more frequently. This struggle is not uncommon for couples with children who must regularly fight to find time to be alone together. But that does not explain the matter entirely. I suspect that our difficulties praying together stem from our significantly different approaches to prayer. My wife is a convert to Catholicism and was raised with a spontaneous and improvisational style of prayer quite different from my own background in which prayer meant "saying prayers." These different styles are evident even in the ways we pray with our children. I am more inclined to introduce our children to the traditional prayers with which I was raised, while she is more likely to pray with them spontaneously or to lead our family in *ad hoc* prayer services at key family celebrations. Over the years of our married life, our approaches to prayer have certainly changed. Diana has moved to a more contemplative style of prayer while my own prayer has been shaped more and more by the liturgy of the Church. We are both, I believe, persons of prayer but we have yet to find a common style of prayer that is equally fulfilling. Our situation certainly does not fit the experience of every married couple. I know several couples who have found ways to make common prayer the centerpiece of their marriage. For us, common prayer continues to be a "work in progress."

I suspect that my decision not to give more attention to prayer in marriage has also been motivated by a discomfort with the way in which many Christians speak of prayer in quantitative terms, as if one's spirituality is measured by the amount of time one commits to prayer. As Teilhard de Chardin observed, this approach dooms most Christians to a second-class status. I value the monastic vocation, but I do not believe that monks live any closer to God than do married couples. That is because I do not believe that prayer is a way of inserting God into our world as if God were otherwise absent. The struggle in the spiritual life is generally not a matter of God's absence but ours. Prayer plays a vital role in any spirituality, not as a measure of God's presence but as a conscious practice that helps us to cultivate a heightened appreciation of the God who is always present to us.

Finally, I would like to offer a word or two about marital fidelity. We trumpet the importance of faithfulness in marriage, as we should, yet we so quickly reduce it to a negative value—not committing adultery. Fidelity is, in a sense, what theologians refer to as an *eschatological virtue*, that is, a virtue that can only be perfectly realized in the glory of the *eschaton* (the divine restructuring of humanity at the end of time); it is something we aspire to as much as it is something that we experience as a present reality. Fidelity is perhaps the most fundamental challenge we face in our marriage, and none of us is completely up to it. One of the most moving moments in our own married life came when Diana and I participated in a Retrouvaille weekend for couples experiencing difficulties in their marriage. Our twin careers and our children had left us little time for each other. Our marriage was not in threat of dissolution, but it had begun to atrophy, as muscles do from too little exercise.

On the weekend we encountered couples who humbled us with the courage they exemplified as they sought to overcome alcoholism, substance abuse, and multiple affairs. This was no warm, fuzzy retreat; this was, for many of these couples, the last lifeline in a drowning marriage. Fidelity took on new meaning for us that weekend. It no longer meant simply an unblemished marital record in which one could proudly profess never having cheated on one's spouse. Many of these couples were dealing with adultery. No, fidelity was evoked in the way these couples refused to quit on each other. Fidelity was not something they either possessed or did not; it was something they aspired to, something they clung to as the only thing that separated their broken relationship from the pragmatic romantic arrangements they had experienced prior to their marriage.

Many couples will never experience the horrible damage that an affair can inflict on a marriage relationship, but no married couple will be exempt from the pain caused by the less significant yet still dangerous exits we make from the demands of our vows. None of us is perfectly faithful; we drift in and out of the attentiveness and charity that our vows demand. Consequently, we can only roughly approximate what God offers us—perfect, accepting, abiding presence to and for each other. In marriage, true fidelity comes to us as hope and task from out of the future of God who is all-faithful.

The community of married life is founded on the most radical of human actions; two people promise themselves, one to another, each casting their lot with this person for the rest of their lives. These promises are most dangerous; they indeed engage us in a daring undertaking. To remain faithful to these promises is to risk everything. It is to walk a tightrope of marital commitment without a net. It means giving up security, comfort, autonomy, control. To marry and to embrace the fruit of marriage is to choose a very particular and demanding way of salvation. To marry is to submit to a crucible of grace. Here the hammer strikes hot iron often as we are being forged into something new, something noble, something of God.

NOTES

PREFACE

1. Mary Anne McPherson Oliver, "Conjugal Spirituality (or Radical Proximity): A New Form of Contemplation," *Spirituality Today* 43 (Spring 1991): 54.
2. See Michael G. Lawler, *Marriage and Sacrament: A Theology of Christian Marriage* (Collegeville, Minn.: Liturgical Press, 1993); Theodore Mackin, *What Is Marriage? Marriage in the Catholic Church* (New York: Paulist, 1982).

CHAPTER ONE: MARRIAGE AND CULTURE

1. David Matzko McCarthy, *Sex and Love in the Home* (London: SCM Press, 2001).
2. Ibid., 60ff.
3. Niklas Luhmann, *Love as Passion: The Codification of Intimacy* (Stanford, Calif.: Stanford University Press, 1998), 147.
4. Barbara Dafoe Whitehead and David Popenoe, *The State of Our Unions: The Social Health of Marriage in America—2001.* (New Brunswick, N.J.: Rutgers University, 2001). http://marriage.rutgers.edu.
5. Vincent Miller, "Taking Consumer Culture Seriously," *Horizons* 27 (Fall 2000): 282.
6. Ibid., 283.
7. Vincent J. Miller, *Consuming Religion: Christian Faith and Practice in a Consumer Culture* (New York: Continuum, 2004).
8. For an extended reflection on this topic, see Richard R. Gaillardetz, *Transforming Our Days: Spirituality, Community, and Liturgy in a Technological Culture* (New York: Crossroad, 2000).
9. See William Doherty, *Take Back Your Marriage: Sticking Together in a World That Pulls Us Apart* (New York: Guilford Press, 2001).

10. Robert Bellah, Richard Madsen, William M. Sullivan, and Ann Swidler: *The Habits of the Heart* (Berkeley, Calif.: University of California Press, 1996), 121–38.

11. McCarthy, 85–108; Mary Howell, *Helping Ourselves: Families and the Human Network* (Boston: Beacon Press, 1975); Edward Shorter, *The Making of the Modern Family* (New York: Basic Books, 1997).

12. Howell, 71.

13. McCarthy, 94.

14. Robert D. Putnam, *Bowling Alone: The Collapse and Revival of American Community*, revised edition (New York: Simon and Schuster, 2000).

15. Miller McPherson, Lynn Smith-Lovin, and Matthew E. Brashears, "Social Isolation in America: Changes in Core Discussion Networks over Two Decades," *American Sociological Review* 71 (June 2006): 353–75.

CHAPTER TWO: MARRIAGE AND FAITH

1. Saint Augustine, *Confessions*, Book 1, Chapter 1.

2. Jean LeClercq, "Introduction," in *Bernard of Clairvaux: Selected Works*, trans. G.R. Evans (New York: Paulist, 1987), 42.

3. The Pastoral Constitution on the Church in the Modern World, 22; translation taken from Austin Flannery, ed., *Vatican Council II: Constitutions, Decrees, Declaration* (Northport, N.Y.: Costello, 1996).

4. These modest inferences about Jesus' "hidden years" depend on John P. Meier, *A Marginal Jew: Rethinking the Historical Jesus* (New York: Doubleday, 1991), 1:278–349.

5. References to "brothers and sisters" of one kind or another appear in the following: Mark 3:31–35, 6:3; Matthew 13:55; Acts 12:17; 15:13; 21:18; 1 Corinthians 15:7; Galatians 1:19, 2:9, 12; James 1:1; Jude 1.

6. Ronald Rolheiser, *The Holy Longing: The Search for a Christian Spirituality* (New York: Doubleday, 1999), 146.

7. Pierre Teilhard de Chardin, *The Divine Milieu* (New York: Harper & Row, 1969), 65–66.

8. I hasten to add that the evangelical witness of committed celibacy itself is a great gift to the Church. I am writing here only of distorted viewpoints.

9. Thomas Merton, *New Seeds of Contemplation* (New York: New Direction Books, 1961), 21.

10. John D. Zizioulas, *Being as Communion: Studies in Personhood and the Church* (Crestwood, N.Y.: St. Vladimir's Seminary Press, 1985).

11. Michael Downey, *Altogether Gift: A Trinitarian Spirituality* (Maryknoll, N.Y.: Orbis, 2001), 45.

CHAPTER THREE: MARRIAGE
AND THE LIFE OF COMMUNION

1. Kallistos Ware, "The Sacrament of Love: The Orthodox Understanding of Marriage and Its Breakdown," *Downside Review* (April 1991): 79.
2. Stephen H. Webb, *The Gifting God: A Trinitarian Ethics of Excess* (New York: Oxford University Press, 1996), 93.
3. My reading of this text draws from the analysis of Michael G. Lawler, *Secular Marriage, Christian Sacrament* (Mystic, Conn.: Twenty-Third Publications, 1985), 11–18.
4. Markus Barth, *Ephesians: Introduction, Translation, and Commentary on Chapters 1–3* (New York: Doubleday, 1974), 618.
5. Evelyn Eaton Whitehead and James D. Whitehead, *Marrying Well: Stages on the Journey of Christian Marriage* (Garden City, N.Y.: Doubleday, 1981), 227.
6. Ibid.
7. This felicitous phrase is drawn from the journal of Etty Hillesum, *An Interrupted Life and Letters from Westerbork* (New York: Holt, 1983), 231.

CHAPTER FOUR: MARRIAGE AND CONVERSION

1. Nancy Mairs, *Ordinary Time: Cycles in Marriage, Faith, and Renewal* (Boston: Beacon Press, 1993), 106.
2. Rolheiser, 196.
3. Augustus Napier, *The Fragile Bond: In Search of an Equal, Intimate, and Enduring Marriage* (New York: Harper & Row, 1988).
4. Ibid., 14.
5. Paul Palmer, "Christian Marriage: Contract or Covenant?" *Theological Studies* 33 (1972): 639.
6. Andre Dubus, "On Charon's Wharf," in *Broken Vessels* (Boston: D.R. Godine, 1991), 80–81.
7. Nick Hornby, *High Fidelity* (New York: Riverhead Books, 1995).
8. Ibid., 273.
9. Ibid., 274.
10. Ibid., 241.
11. Ibid., 314–15.
12. Ibid., 318.

13. Rainer Maria Rilke, *Letters to a Young Poet*, revised ed. (New York: Norton, 1954), 53–54, 57–58.

14. Michael Leunig, *A Common Prayer* (North Blackburn, Australia: Collins Dove, 1990).

CHAPTER FIVE: MARRIAGE AND SEXUALITY

1. Karol Wojtyla, *Love and Responsibility* (New York: Farrar, Straus & Giroux, 1981), 270–78.

2. Phyllis Trible, *God and the Rhetoric of Sexuality* (Philadelphia: Fortress Press, 1978), 72–147.

3. Karen Lebacqz, "Appropriate Vulnerability: A Sexual Ethic for Singles," *Christian Century* 104 (1987): 435–38.

4. Ibid., 437.

5. Luke Timothy Johnson, "A Disembodied 'Theology of the Body,'" *Commonweal* (January 26, 2001): 15.

6. This treatment of *eros* is drawn from Richard Westley, "Marriage, Sexuality and Spirituality," *Chicago Studies* 32 (November 1993): 214–21.

7. Saint Thomas of Aquinas, *Summa Theologiae I*, q. 98, a. 2. For a comparison of the approaches of Augustine and Aquinas on sexuality, see Andre Guindon, *The Sexual Language: An Essay in Moral Theology* (Ottawa: University of Ottawa Press, 1977), 68ff.

8. Saint Thomas of Aquinas, *Summa Theologiae II-II*, q. 153, a. 2 ad 2.

9. Guindon, 70.

10. Pope Benedict XVI, *God Is Love* (*Deus Caritas Est*), 5, Vatican City: Libreria Editrice Vaticana, December 25, 2005.

11. Ibid., 7–8.

12. Cristina L.H. Traina, "Papal Ideals, Marital Realities: One View from the Ground," in *Sexual Diversity and Catholicism*, eds., Patricia Jung and J. Coray, (Collegeville, Minn.: Liturgical Press, 1989), 269–87, at 273.

13. Mitch Finley, "The Dark Side of Natural Family Planning," *America* (February 23, 1991): 207.

14. Oliver, 63–66.

15. Ibid., 63.

16. Pope John Paul II, *The Theology of the Body: Human Love in the Divine Plan* (Boston: Pauline Media, 1997). For a systematic exposition of the pope's theology of the body, see Christopher West, *Theology of the Body Explained: A Commentary on John Paul II's "Gospel of the Body"* (Boston: Pauline Books and Media, 2003).

17. David Matzko McCarthy, *Sex and Love in the Home* (London: SCM, 2001), 8.

18. Vigen Guroian, *Incarnate Love: Essays in Orthodox Ethics* (Notre Dame, Ind.: University of Notre Dame Press, 1987), 31.

19. Second Vatican Council: The Pastoral Constitution on the Church in the Modern World *(Gaudium et Spes)*, 48, December 7, 1965.

20. Ibid., 50.

21. The crucial sections regarding the morality of artificial birth regulation and the liceity of natural family planning are found in Pope Paul VI, On Human Life *(Humanae Vitae)*, 14–16, July 25, 1968.

22. See Gaillardetz, *Transforming Our Days*.

23. Finley, "The Dark Side of Natural Family Planning," 206–7.

24. Traina, 278.

25. Julie Hanlon Rubio, "Beyond the Liberal/Conservative Divide on Contraception: The Wisdom of Practitioners of Natural Family Planning and Artificial Birth Control," *Horizons* 32/2 (2005): 270–94, at 278.

26. For more guidance on how Catholics are to respond in circumstances where they struggle to accept official Church teaching, see Richard R. Gaillardetz, *By What Authority? A Primer on Scripture, the Magisterium and the Sense of the Faithful* (Collegeville, Minn.: Liturgical Press, 2003), chapter 8.

CHAPTER SIX: MARRIAGE AND THE DOMESTIC CHURCH

1. This material on the domestic church was previously published, in a revised form as "The Church as Domestic," in *The Marks of the Church*, eds. William Madges and Michael J. Daley (Mystic, Conn.: Twenty-Third Publications, 2006).

2. See William R. Herzog II, *Parables as Subversive Speech: Jesus as Pedagogue of the Oppressed* (Louisville, Ky.: Westminster/Knox, 1994).

3. Stephen Post, "Adoption Theologically Considered," *Journal of Religious Ethics* (Spring 1997): 149–68.

4. United States Conference of Catholic Bishops, "Follow the Way of Love," *Origins* 23 (December 2, 1993): 436.

5. José de Mesa, *Marriage Is Discipleship* (Quezon City, Philippines: East Asian Pastoral Institute, 1995), 128–33.

6. Christine Pohl, *Making Room: Recovering Hospitality as a Christian Tradition* (Grand Rapids, Mich.: Eerdmans, 1999).

7. Ibid., 62.

8. Mesa, 133.

9. See Jean Vanier, *Community and Growth* (New York: Paulist Press, 1989); Michael Downey, *A Blessed Weakness: The Spirit of Jean Vanier and l'Arche* (San Francisco: Harper & Row, 1986).

10. International Committee on English in the Liturgy, *The Roman Missal* (Washington, DC: United States Catholic Conference, Inc., 1973).

11. Pope John Paul II, On Human Work (*Laborem Exercens*), September 14, 1981.

12. Julie Hanlon Rubio, *A Christian Theology of Marriage and Family* (New York: Paulist Press, 2003).

13. Ibid.

14. My thoughts on forgiveness have been enriched by L. Gregory Jones, *Embodying Forgiveness: A Theological Analysis* (Grand Rapids, Mich.: Eerdmans, 1995).

EPILOGUE

1. Thomas Merton, *New Seeds of Contemplation* (Norfolk: New Directions, 1961), 31–32.

SUGGESTED READING

Bourg, Florence Caffrey. *Where Two or Three Are Gathered: Christian Families as Domestic Churches*. Notre Dame, Ind.: University of Notre Dame Press, 2004.

Callahan, Sidney. *Parents Forever: You and Your Adult Children*. New York: Crossroad, 1992.

Doherty, William. *Take Back Your Marriage: Sticking Together in a World That Pulls Us Apart*. New York: Guilford Press, 2001.

Donnelly, Dody. *Radical Love: An Approach to Sexual Spirituality*. Minneapolis: Winston Press, 1984.

Ferder, Fran, and John Heagle. *Your Sexual Self: Pathway to Authentic Intimacy*. Notre Dame, Ind.: Ave Maria Press, 1992.

Gallagher, Charles A., George A. Maloney, S.J., and Paul F. Wilczak. *Embodied in Love: Sacramental Spirituality and Sexual Intimacy*. New York: Crossroad, 1984.

Guindon, Andre. *The Sexual Language: An Essay in Moral Theology*. Ottawa: University of Ottawa Press, 1977.

Kasper, Walter. *Theology of Christian Marriage*. New York: Crossroad, 1981.

Lawler, Michael G. *Marriage and Sacrament: A Theology of Christian Marriage*. Collegeville, Minn.: Liturgical Press, 1993.

_____. *Secular Marriage, Christian Sacrament*. Mystic, Conn.: Twenty-Third Publications, 1992.

Mackin, Theodore. *What Is Marriage? Marriage in the Catholic Church*. New York: Paulist, 1982.

Mairs, Nancy. *Ordinary Time: Cycles in Marriage, Faith, and Renewal*. Boston: Beacon Press, 1993.

McDonald, Patrick J., and Claudette M. McDonald. *Can Your Marriage Be a Friendship?* New York: Paulist, 1996.

———. *The Soul of a Marriage.* New York: Paulist, 1995.

Mesa, José M. de. *Marriage Is Discipleship.* Quezon City, Philippines: East Asian Pastoral Institute, 1995.

Napier, Augustus. *The Fragile Bond: In Search of an Equal, Intimate, and Enduring Marriage.* New York: Harper & Row, 1988.

Roberts, William P. *Commitment to Partnership: Explorations of the Theology of Marriage.* New York: Paulist, 1987.

Roberts, William P., and Michael G. Lawler, eds. *Christian Marriage and Family: Contemporary Theological and Pastoral Perspectives.* Collegeville, Minn.: Liturgical Press, 1996.

Rubio, Julie Hanlon. *A Christian Theology of Marriage and Family.* New York: Paulist, 2003.

Salzman, Todd A., Thomas M. Kelly, and John J. O'Keefe, eds. *Marriage in the Catholic Tradition.* New York: Crossroad, 2004.

Schillebeeckx, Edward. *Marriage: Secular Reality and Saving Mystery.* New York: Sheed & Ward, 1965.

Tetlow, Elisabeth Meier, and Louis Mulry Tetlow. *Partners in Service: Toward a Biblical Theology of Christian Marriage.* Lanham, Md.: University Press of America, 1983.

Thomas, David M. *Christian Marriage: A Journey Together.* Wilmington, Del.: Glazier, 1983.

Trible, Phyllis. *God and the Rhetoric of Sexuality.* Philadelphia: Fortress Press, 1978.

Whitehead, Evelyn Eaton, and James D. Whitehead. *Marrying Well: Stages on the Journey of Christian Marriage.* Garden City, N.Y.: Doubleday, 1981.

Witte, John Jr. *From Sacrament to Contract: Marriage, Religion, and Law in the Western Tradition.* Louisville, Ky.: Westminster John Knox Press, 1997.

CPSIA information can be obtained
at www.ICGtesting.com
Printed in the USA
FFOW04n1928071117
43404727-42019FF